The Human Experience

Life as We (Don't Really) Know It

Elizabeth Crooks

ISBN: 0692573011

ISBN-13: 978-0692573013

Cover by Elizabeth Crooks

For more information please visit:

www.elizabeth-crooks.com

DEDICATION

To all who are remembering their brilliance in every moment:
Keep remembering. Keep expanding your possibilities. Find your
truth and live it.

TABLE OF CONTENTS

"A human being is a part of the whole called by us universe, a part limited in time and space. He experiences himself, his thoughts and feeling as something separated from the rest, a kind of optical delusion of his consciousness. This delusion is a kind of prison for us, restricting us to our personal desires and to affection for a few persons nearest to us. Our task must be to free ourselves from this prison by widening our circle of compassion to embrace all living creatures and the whole of nature in its beauty."
- Albert Einstein

PREFACE

In my experience, this is what I have come to understand about the nature of reality and the experience we call life as a human. My intent writing this book is to get you to think, as others have done for me. I can only show you the doors that have opened for me and the knowledge I have come across on my own journey. I share so it may assist others on their own journey.

Truth is relative and subjective: it changes with new knowledge and new understandings. What is true for you in this moment may not be true in the next. We all have to find our own truth, and we expand with every new piece of information that crosses our path. At the very least, use this information to expand your mind. Expand your possibilities. We read to gain knowledge we weren't aware of before. And awareness leads to consciousness.

Take this information as just another theory of life. By no means is it the end all-be all, or the ultimate Truth with a capital 'T'. Find what resonates for you within this information and discard the rest. Please do not substitute the information within this book for professional advice, medical or otherwise. The information within this book is meant to scratch the surface of our perceived reality as human beings living on planet Earth. Delve deeper, ask questions on your own. Only you can find your truth. I hope this helps you on your journey.

INTRODUCTION

Every moment is life changing. Every change is a gift.

In every moment you experience something new. Something that changes the way you think, alters a belief, questions your thoughts, challenges the old ways, enlightens to new possibilities... everything literally changes in a moment. And with moments constantly changing, all that ever exists is change, or growth. Change may seem like a bad thing to the human aspect, but on a higher dimensional level, of the soul and our higher selves, change is welcomed with open arms as an experience; an evolution of universal proportions.

For our lives as humans on a planet called Earth are not for naught: our lives do have meaning. And that meaning is galactic, universal even. Our purpose is to experience new things constantly. Our purpose is to evolve our thinking process, to accept all possibilities in life and beyond life as we know it. We are the universe expressing itself as a human for only a moment.

To view change as a gift is essential to overcoming the earthly or egoic viewpoint that life is meaningless or difficult. The human aspect fears change because it cannot prepare, or attempt to prepare, for what "happens next". We use our past to dictate our future, believing that things only happen in certain ways and that nothing happens the way we want it to. What do we want exactly? And why don't we already have it? Unless, in fact, we already have it and we are, just, simply unware of it.

We've been told we have everything we need inside of us. The human aspect brushes this statement to the side with a snort or a chuckle. Of course we have everything within us; you are referring to our heart and capacity for love beyond all the superficial hardship and life (the hate, the struggles, the lies). The grand deceit is that all struggle, or the mere thought of it, is a lie, an illusion built and designed for one purpose: to experience.

We are galactic star beings. We are the universe. We are more than this shell, this vessel, we call the human body that functions quite well on this plane of existence we call planet Earth. To compact our true nature into a tiny, actually the tiniest, box and label it as life does far more damage than good to our beliefs, the core of our existence.

Beliefs change, in every moment, and constantly too with each new experience. Yes we have everything we need inside of us already. We always have. And always will. For we are pure, unconditional love; pure, star light essence that has chosen to experience itself in a tiny box for only a moment of time in the vastness of the illusion of time itself.

For time is merely an illusion. If it actually exists then it is not as we think it to be. The human mind thinks time is linear, segmented and finite. On a grander, or cosmic, scale, time is cyclical. The universe expresses itself as ages composed of our earthly millennials in which ages come and go to once again reign for their allotted "time". The human aspect views this concept as the science of astrology and horoscope. The sun, the moon and the stars…all dance to a symphony beyond the range of human comprehension and appreciation. Beyond the cosmos, time is what it wants to be. It expresses itself as it sees fit, as an experience in and of itself.

Our time on Earth, in a human shell, is limited compared to our true nature: infinite beings infinitely expressing themselves throughout infinite galaxies and worlds designed with the highest good and purpose in mind: infinite experience.

Experience is the true commodity of the universe. To the soul, our higher selves, experience is the purpose to life itself. For life expresses itself in many forms. This lifetime we are as humans who experience working menial jobs to exchange paper and coin for food, comfort and other pleasures. Simultaneously we are other humanoid creatures on similar planets in neighboring galaxies expressing life in alternate fashions. When this ride is over, when the game ends, we will move on to the next ride, start a new game, in order to gather more experience.

We chose this, as our higher selves. We wanted to experience life as a human being on this planet with its certain characteristics and limited parameters. The game of life has rules. We chose to participate in these rules until we remembered that we were playing a game in the first place. Once we remember, we can choose differently. For choice is all we have.

The game is changing as the age of the planet, the galaxy, changes. Once a lower dimensional planet with strict rules for advancement, yet ripe with learning opportunities, the Earth is evolving into a higher dimensional planet, equipping itself for a different kind of experience; a new journey in which the human being remembers its divinity and can choose to express it and experience in new ways never before conceived by the limited human mind.

Human life may seem tiny in comparison to the vastness of the universe and our true nature, but to the soul, our higher selves, being human is one of the noblest things to accomplish. We should feel gratitude and appreciation for our lives spent as humans. For it is as if the Earth is a once-in-a-lifetime epic rock concert, a universally-renowned play, or a soul's kindergarten graduation celebration with a line wrapped around the cosmos, with every manner of essence waiting for their turn to experience it.

Human life is precious, epic even, when compared to the vastness of its true nature: experience. Humanity is ripe with experience. That is why many of us choose to come to Earth to play over and over again. And when we are done with this planet we move on to a new experience somewhere else, with a new concept of "time" and life "purpose". Humanity struggles to find purpose because it searches without itself instead of within itself. The heart is the seat of the soul; our true selves. And when our hearts are open to receive the new, the change, and the experiences, our souls are as light as a feather made of pure light itself.

Every experience is a gift. The egoic mind will attempt to label it, compartmentalize it, pick it apart and judge it. The soul loves and accepts all as pure love and light, for that is all it is and ever will be, in time or not. We are love. We are light. The darkness is a gift, for it reminds us that ultimately all that exists within is light, and that the darkness in only an illusion. The fear of change is only an illusion. Judging change is only human. Remember that we are all divine star beings, beyond this human shell.

Enjoy the ride for what it is. Embrace change, for it will show you things you never knew were possible before. Embody love and exude it towards all beings, creatures on this planet. But most of all, experience everything.

PART ONE:

LIFE AS WE
(DON'T REALLY)
KNOW IT

THE HUMAN EXPERIENCE

"You don't have a soul, you are a soul. You have a body."
- C.S Lewis

We are souls having a human experience, not humans having a spiritual experience. To think of ourselves as just human is limiting our true potential. As souls we are the entire universe, we are a part of the whole. Humanity has separated itself off from this knowledge. The human aspect has grown to fear "what happens next" because it cannot truly understand that there is no such thing as death if we are infinite souls having a human experience for just a moment. As souls we get to experience many different forms of life and existence over the vastness of the universe on a myriad of planets in infinite galaxies. Earth is simply a game. Earth is just a story we've created and are reenacting like a play on a theatre stage. When we are done playing this game, when we are done with the story, we move onto a new one.

So let's talk about this experience we call "Human"...

The first thing to remember is that we chose this experience. We chose the game, and we agreed to the rules. In fact, we wanted to come here so bad that there is a waiting list to get onto the Earth at this time! Many souls desire to jump onto this ship we call Earth, especially at this time of ascension and a paradigm shift in consciousness.

This is a unique opportunity to experience physical ascension alongside a planetary ascension, and so if you are reading this right now you are one of the luckiest souls to have this experience at this time.

So why don't we remember that we are playing a game when we arrive? Because that is also a part of the rules that we agreed to in order to come to planet Earth and live through a human vessel. We chose to experience density, which gives us a sort of amnesia as we are immersed fully into the illusion of life as a human. If you knew you were playing a game, would you have experienced everything you have so far? Would you even want to play the game after all you have been through? That is why the veils are in place, so we can fully experience and grow from our lives in a human body without the knowledge that we are more than human.

But the rules of the game have changed. Since December 2012 or when the Mayan Calendar predicted "the end of the world," the veils have been slowly lifting as the Earth and humanity enters a new age of ascension. So in a sense, the world did end on December 21, 2012: the world as we knew it and had been playing for centuries. It was time for a new game with new rules and so here we are, remembering our true potential and knowledge of things beyond the scope of a simple life on planet Earth.

Life doesn't seem as complicated or as stressful when you consider that it is just a game. But what is the purpose of the game? As souls we like to gather as much experience as possible so we can learn and grow from each experience. But what is the purpose of life to the human aspect? Certainly there is more to life than just having things happen to us and seeing our reaction to those things. What is the human supposed to do for human's sake? I believe it is to share our selves and our creativities with the world.

Earth is an open playground. Are we meant to just pay bills and die? That is part of the game we signed up for, yes, but there is more to it. The Earth is a natural housing for many different beings, a host for plant and animal life, a planet for travel and exploration, and it facilitates the exchange of knowledge. Humans are naturally receptive to this knowledge, although we have forgotten how to access it over thousands of years of playing a certain game. The human experience can be more than what we've always thought it to be, we just have to start thinking outside the box…well, actually, realizing that there is no box to begin with!

Many people feel like they are here for a reason. This reason doesn't have to be life-altering. Maybe our reason for being here is to assist another with their journey. There is a reason why you went to the grocery store when you did. There is a reason why you were stuck in a traffic jam on the way to the hospital. We just don't know the "why" things happen until after they happen. There are grander reasons why we do the things we do, even the little things.
The grander design of all things is to further our individual journeys, complete soul contracts and to gain as much experience as we can in one human lifetime, even if we have no idea what we are doing in our lives at this moment.

Everyone has a role to play in the fabric of reality. We all have our parts. We are all here for ourselves, and we are also here for one another as a collective. What makes the game interesting is the question: "How should I do it this time?" What role do you want to play? And even if you were born into a certain role, you have the ability to change how you want to play at any time. See life as a role-playing-game; notice what other people around you are doing and think about why they are doing it, what role are they playing in your life? What role are you playing in their life?

When you start to notice the patterns you can start to piece together your life plan and discover your purpose. Just don't get hung up on thinking you need a purpose; life is often experience enough. What if this is all you get? Can you get okay with that? What if what you are destined for is happening at this moment, nothing more, nothing less: can you get okay with that?

Nothing has meaning or importance. We've temporarily given it meaning as a part of the virtual experience, and as an experience in and of itself. The soul doesn't judge an experience; it doesn't expect to have a certain one a certain way. And while the soul plans out what it wants to experience and learn this time playing the game, free will contributes to the infinite possibilities in how lessons are actually played out throughout our lives.

If there is just one main lesson we are all working on at this moment, it is the discovery of self-love. Not learning self-love, because we know we are already pure love as souls, as divine beings. The human aspect just forgot about self-love while playing the game. And since the game is changing, humanity is discovering more and more about its true potential as pure love in every moment.

The human experience is a choice. We chose to come here to play and we can choose how we want to continue to play the game. Remember that everything around you is for you to play with. Everything is a learning experience, even if it doesn't feel that good. Just play with the possibilities. Play with your food, play with your body, play with your thoughts, and play with every part of your experience. Play with every story that comes up! We are each in charge of our own experience, and we are only going to have the experience that we have agreed to have, even if that means saying we want to renegotiate the terms of the contract at this moment. We have the power to make a new choice in every moment.

The Non-Human Experience:

Planet Earth is not just a playground for the human race. Animals are also consciously living their lives through experiences and interactions with everything Earth has to offer. Animals are here to assist humanity in many ways, one of which is by acting like mirrors to show us our state of being. When we change our energy, animals respond in turn. As mirrors, basically our need for them makes them need us. When we no longer need animals and pets from an egoic standpoint, they will no longer need us in the same way, i.e. dependency.

Animals have had the ability to feel vibrational energy because they don't have the filters of the human mind. And it is because of this ability that they can assist us on an unconscious level. Dogs have agreed to be our companions and absorb our negative energies. Cats are here to help dogs transmute that energy because they can handle a bit more than dogs and have made a contract with them to assist in that aspect.

Cats also have contracts with humans. They mainly assist in getting the human aspect present in the moment. Cats in particular connect with and see energy on a higher spectrum than humans, often seeing spirits and interacting with energetic beings

21

beyond the perception of the human senses.

Likewise, there are many different races of beings throughout the universe that exist in a different energetic spectrum than what the human aspect is accustomed to experiencing. Many races are coexisting here on planet Earth in various dimensions and timelines that are running parallel to the human existence.

If you are not having a human experience, you may be having one of these experiences in which your soul has chosen a vessel for a particular experience this moment in time, on this planet or another:

Sirians, Lyrans, Atlanteans, Angels, Merpeople, Lemurians, The Annunaki, Reptilians, Elves, Dwarves, Dragons, Elementals (Sylphs, Undines, Salamanders and Gnomes), Unicorns, Faeries, The Jinn, Dryads, Halflings, The Formless, Carians, The Elohim, Andarians, Andromedans, Celestials, Arcturians, Pterodactyls, The Greys, Leviathans, Martians, Aryans/Orions, The Mu, Insectoids, Vampires, Werewolves, Nymphs, Gargoyles, Menehune, The Nameless, Pleiadians, Humanoids, Dolphins, Zombies, Venusians, Dinosaurs, The Bees, Demons, Robots, The Shape-Shifters, Devas, and of course The Yetis.
(…and many more)

THE CONTRACT

"An invisible thread connects those who are destined to meet, regardless of time, place, and circumstance. The thread may stretch or tangle. But it will never break."
-Ancient Chinese Proverb

First, let us go over some basic information regarding the Soul:

As a human, our Soul would be considered our "higher self" (higher in the sense that our soul has already ascended through the hierarchy of consciousness, not that the soul is in any way better or more advanced from an egoic standpoint). As Souls we have continued to fragment and fragment from Source to experience life in its infinite possibilities.

So basically we have ourselves, as an individualized Soul, connected to all other Souls because we all come from the same Source. Our individualized Soul is made up of two halves (we refer to this as our twin soul, or the other half of us). Those two halves belong to a cluster called a Soul Family which is made up of 11 other Souls with one main Oversoul at the center. This is one cluster that is connected to another cluster of 12 which come together into one...and so forth. Ultimately there are 144,000 Soul groupings that form the basis of all the fragments of Source, each unique and part of the whole at the same time.

Essentially, there are twelve of you living at the same "time." These other parts of you may be living on different planets or on the same planet in different situations for a maximum amount of life experience. And with twin souls taken into account, there are really 24 of us living simultaneously.

Sometimes we get glimpses into our other lives when we visit the dream world or have some sort of out-of-body experience, or when we are induced with certain drugs that allow the veils between worlds to thin. The one "you" that you are aware of, the one living this life you are experiencing, is unique and self-sustaining. Most people don't ever meet their other aspects in a lifetime unless it was under contract to do so. All of these different aspects of our one-self exist to provide the maximum amount of experience per person, per lifetime (which adds up to an infinite amount of experience overall).

So now that I have blown your mind...

What are Soul Contracts?

Our contracts, or soul contracts, are with our higher selves, other selves, soul families, soul tribes and Source consciousness itself. It is our contracts that give life experiences through interaction with others on a multi-dimensional playing field.

Although we planned out our game of life, including all the major players and most of the minor ones to fulfill certain contracts at certain times, when we got to Earth we forgot all the rules of the game and all the stuff we had planned out for us. And we decided that this was going to be fun...

Contracts can span the course of "time" which is the human lifespan. Contracts can initiate and complete within a fraction of a second as well. Have you ever said something to someone that was so out of character you had no idea where that thought came from? That was your higher-self completing its contract with another's higher-self in that moment. It could have been one word, just one single word, that that person needed to experience in order to complete a part of its soul work on Earth. Contracts have no parameters other than to assist in the utmost good and well-being of all life and purpose.

Once you start to recognize the soul contracts within your life you can start to affect them consciously. Families are our first soul contracts on Earth. Our parents were contracted out, carefully selected for the type of experience we wanted during our Earth lives. Yes, we planned out everything with our parents...how they would treat us, what they would teach us, what thoughts and beliefs they would implant within us by the time we were adults...we chose the backdrop of our human life before we were even born. After we were "grown" we would have everything within us to work out and decipher the code of our lives and unravel the experience to find the core lesson or theme to our existence this time around.

When you find that core theme, you can choose to end contracts prematurely if you believe you have learned the necessary lessons from that experience (i.e. if your primary caregiver instilled worthlessness throughout early childhood, finding self-worth and recognizing the triggers your caregivers bring up in you regarding worth could be an indication of a contract fulfilling itself). Not all contracts can be fulfilled from a third dimensional egoic standpoint though. On the surface the contract may appear complete, but new contracts and additions could be made behind the scenes for future lessons and experiences.

To the soul, experience is everything. It does not matter in which form it takes. Some experiences are specifically sought, yes, but life has infinite possibilities in which to express such experiences. Every life is unique. Every experience is unique.

Every human has experiences, most of which are of a central theme, but the manner in which they are expressed, in each individual across time periods and generations, is the beauty of life; the beauty of possibility and infinite expressions of each experience. As with life, contracts can change in any moment, if it is necessary or of the utmost good. Good, not in the sense of good and bad or right and wrong, but as supportive and beneficial.

Life is more than a contract. Life is what you make it between the lines, and beyond the fine print. Enjoy the experience for what it is: unconditional love experiencing all manners of conditions, parameters, limiting beliefs, boxes and hurdles to overcome…and just for the experience of it.

Twin Souls, Soul Mates and Twin Flames

Twin Souls are the other half of your soul. Most people never meet up with their twin soul in their lifetime. However, more and more twin souls are coming together because they do work together on an energetic level during the ascension process. We basically have split our soul in two to experience twice as many things within the same parameters. Remember that each individual life is unique. If two people grew up in the same household with the same experiences, they would still look at a tree and see something slightly different because of their own unique brain pattern. What we see as other people outside of ourselves, whether they are family, friends, or strangers, are actually just other aspects of ourselves.

There is a difference between twin souls and soul mates. Soul mates are simply souls that you have made an agreement with. You have reincarnated in other lifetimes with each other and you have agreed to come in together at different points in each other's lives to play out a certain role. This is to assist you in breaking out of your comfort zone and getting you un-stuck from the programs of everyday life. Do they need to be with you for you to make progress? Absolutely not.

Everything is in perfect timing. You will meet them, and they will be in your life as long as they need to be, and then they will move on. Soul mates can be random strangers on the street that say just one word to you in passing. As long as they are assisting and completing contracts, they were destined to be in your life.

The human aspect thinks it has one true soul mate that it will be incomplete without. This is not the case. We have many agreements and many souls come into many people's lives. There is no such thing as needing to be complete as part of the game of life. We are all whole, always. When twin souls split, they are living life simultaneously, not separately.

As long as you don't trust yourself, you will seek someone "out there" to tell you what you need to hear and to confirm what you do or do not believe. People in our lives are mirrors, soul mates are mirrors. They will either tell you something you do or don't agree with, or to activate/trigger a fear, or to question what you already believe, and many more. The human aspect needs to verify its truth while the soul trusts that it has everything it needs to know within itself.

While soul mates are here to simply complete contracts, twin flames more accurately describe the relationship between two

27

people, two souls, in relation to the human's notion of a soul mate. However, a twin flame relationship is not about sex; that is a human thing. Twin flames come together to support and trigger each other.

Triggering refers to eliciting a response through any form of action. Two people in a relationship will often push each other's buttons: this is a form of triggering. Triggering to the Soul is just an experience to get over, or to get okay, with something happening. If someone keeps calling you ugly or worthless, triggering an emotional response within you, your soul may want to learn self-worth by figuring out that it doesn't matter what other people say about you.

Whatever your path may be, it is for you to figure out why you react the way you to do other people and things happening in your life. One way to think about twin flames is that they ignite the "flame" within us by triggering an anger response, etc.

I like to think of the phrase "Namaste" to mean "my soul recognizes your soul." Appreciate the soul mates and twin flames that enter your life. We learn something new from everyone we meet. Not every contract will be an intimate relationship. Most of the time contracts are with our friends or as a passing hello to someone you recognize that you have spent other lifetimes with on some level of experience.

Those people looking and waiting for a lover may miss out on their one and only chance encounter with their twin flame in this lifetime. We cannot see what we are not looking for, especially when we are focused on something else; a particular outcome for instance. Keep your hearts open for new experiences. Release attachments and expectations and everything will just fall into place.

LIVING NEUTRALITY

"The root of suffering is attachment"
-Buddha

The concept of neutrality is foreign to the human aspect, or the Ego. Taking a neutral approach to life's experiences is of the soul's domain, for there is no right or wrong, no good and bad, no positives and negatives in the universe. Duality is of the old paradigm, a game humanity has played out for millennium, and that game has so-far ended.

To see everything as just an experience is neutrality. To believe everything is just an experience is living neutrality. How can every experience be neither good nor bad? Getting hit by a fast-moving car can be pretty bad for a human. Winning a five hundred million dollar jackpot can be pretty good for a human. Both experiences are perfect in their own way. That is the essence of experience; it is just that, experience.

The human aspect can get caught up in duality and polarity: everything is either positive or negative. If you don't want to have a bad day, you try and think positive: "look on the bright side!" However, our true state is to be neutral and not to say things like "the glass is half-full" or "the glass is half-empty." If you have a glass, and it is filled with some manner of liquid, then that is amazing in and of itself. I am glad to have a glass that contains water for me to drink and I don't need to judge how much or how little water I have in this moment.

Instead of seeing things as good and bad or right and wrong, you can choose to see things as they are. "It is what it is. This is what is playing out in my reality right now." Be an open platform. Realize you have chosen that software program. The glass may only be half-full, but you don't have to see it as half-empty. You don't even have to measure it at all. Everything is perfect, and everything is as it is meant to be.

Neutrality is not about not caring. We care, but we don't carry it around with us. We get okay with what is happening. We get okay with what we have. There are no mistakes in the universe. But everything is not there to always remain in our world. When you get to a certain level of consciousness, and you have learned what you needed to learn, things no longer serve their purpose. And so you move onto a new chapter in your life's story, a new state of experience. So if the props and the staging for a particular play are no longer necessary because you have moved on to creating a new show, then guess what? That stage and those props become obsolete and you take it down to put up a new one. As things get completed and experiences become obsolete, they are dissolved from your reality.

Being neutral is about going with the flow. "This is what I do now." This doesn't mean that this is what you have to do five seconds from now, or keep doing for the rest of your life. Do what you feel guided to do. Be open to new experiences. There are no requirements to do something of value or to do something that makes you feel a certain way. Live moment to moment. We came here to experience. We came here to play. There is no future and no past, only now. We feel lost when we think we should be doing something. Everything changes so quickly that knowing the future only limits you. Only the human aspect cares about "what happens next."

Expectations and Attachments:

Each moment is creating the next moment only. No one can truly plan for the future. The human aspect fears the future because, as of right now, there is no future, or at least no consistent future, no designated future. We expect there to be a future. We want to have a particular kind of future. And the human can get attached to that particular future and constantly feel angry or depressed when that future never comes.

Thoughts and emotions are created when our expected reality is different from actual reality. Expectations attach emotions to outcomes. If I don't get this then I'll be angry, sad or happy. If this happens, or that happens, then I'll feel this way or that way. Not only do we become attached to physical objects, but we attach our own perceptions and ideals onto other people as well. We project our expectations onto others. And we are often disappointed when those people are not who we want them to be.

The goal is to get okay with anything that is happening at any moment. So you expected someone to apologize and they didn't. You expected that guy to not cut you off in traffic. You expected to have your favorite muffin waiting for you at the local coffee shop on your way to work and it wasn't there.

If you are only going to be happy if all the pieces of your life fit into a neat little box of your own limited design, well then you are never going to be happy. Our expectations in life, and our attachments to certain outcomes, rarely equal what actually happens. Ride the ride, play along in the play. Happiness is letting go of the expectations and enjoying what is, for what it is.

Judgments:

No one likes to be judged. In fact, many fears derive from the fear of judgment. If you think you live a life without judgment, think again. We all judge, but mostly we don't realize it, and here is why: opinion = judgment. If you have an opinion about something, you are in fact judging it. Some judgment is obvious, but most of the time it is subtle. Our subtle judgments shine a light on the underlying thoughts about ourselves and our lives. Little comments, opinions, about daily things tell us how we think and what we think. Opinions tell us where our expectations and attachments are.

When you think about your daily routine, what are you thinking about? Is it a nice day out? Is it too cloudy, or too sunny, for you? Maybe you didn't like that shade of blue on that car when it passed you on the street. Maybe the trashcan at the office was too full for your liking. Every little opinion equates to some underlying judgment. Perhaps you would have chosen a different color of that car, and perhaps someone wasn't doing their job well enough to empty the trashcan when you thought it should be emptied.

All we can do is work with our thoughts, really hear what we are saying about ourselves and the world around us, and decide if we want to continue to think that way in this moment. Neutrality is a choice, and it takes some practice to see through one's expectations, attachments and judgements in their reality.

THE FOUR BODIES OF CONSCIOUSNESS

"Waking up to who you are requires letting go of who you imagine yourself to be."
- Alan W. Watts

Consciousness is defined as the state of awareness of one's own existence within their surroundings. It has also been defined as: sentience, the ability to experience or to feel, wakefulness, and having a sense of selfhood. Consciousness connotes the relationship between the mind and the external world, as well as the relationship between the mind and God, or the relationship between the mind and the deeper truths that are thought to be more fundamental than the physical world.

As individuals, we each have our own consciousness. More specifically, we each have four bodies of consciousness: our physical body, our mental body, our emotional body, and our soul body. These are the four aspects of self. Each has a specific function, unique goals and contracts, and their own way of communicating. In addition to individual consciousness, we are all a part of a collective consciousness, or group consciousness. And there are many clusters of group consciousness, allowing everyone to be a part of more than one at the same time. Countries or larger areas of the world share a certain consciousness. Neighborhoods can share a more localized group consciousness. And then we share a collective consciousness with our soul families within the Earth structure and throughout the universe.

Overall, the collective consciousness of the planet as a whole (i.e. humanity) is not fully ready for the changes that are happening behind the scenes. This is why progress can seem so slow. The group, or the majority of the planet, is not ready for the "Truth"…that we are not alone in the universe, that life as we know it is an illusion, and that we all have the power to change our realities with just a thought. And if we all truly understood and accepted this as a part of our reality, then life as we know it would change in the blink of an eye.

Every single person contributes to the collective consciousness by expanding their own knowledge and by growing as soul, or divine, beings. When enough people want change, when the majority has set their mind to something, then that is when the world changes. It is similar to the 100th monkey effect... just one person can tip the scales by believing a certain way, affecting all belief systems simultaneously. We each have the power to be that 100th monkey and affect social change instantly.

Personal growth and ascension is ultimately achieved by the unification of all four bodies of consciousness. Popular texts describe the trinity of the body, mind and soul paradigm but the mind is actually a split consciousness, as in the two hemispheres.

The mental body is comprised of the ego and is responsible for thought, while the emotional body is comprised of our emotions and reactions as the experiential aspect of thought. All four aspects of consciousness are perfectly designed to give an individual infinite experience, with many factors contributing to each journey with unique physical bodies, belief systems, and emotional reactions based on our individual experience.

I am Not my Body:

Up until this point in time we have generally thought of our body as being who we are. However, with the shift into 4th dimensional consciousness we start to realize that who we really are is Source Itself. And we start to utilize the body as it was originally designed: as just a vehicle. One way to look at is that your body is like a costume your soul puts on so that it can have an experience on this planet. Or, your body is like a rental car in which your soul test drives for a while before deciding it wants to drive a new car on a new road of life.

However you want to view it, the human body is an intricate machine that functions quite well on its own. It heals itself when it gets injured or sick. It breaks down food for nourishment. We didn't get a manual on how to work the human body when we were born...it just started breathing for us and pumping blood and oxygen where it needed to go. We don't have to spend all our time breaking down our meals into protein and sugars, or making sure we keep breathing in every moment. Most of that stuff is automatic, which allows us to experience life in other ways.

We often don't give the physical body enough credit. It keeps us breathing while we sleep of all things! It naturally detoxifies and regenerates all the time. It is the vessel in which we experience life itself. Our essence, our consciousness, is housed within the body and we sense the world around us through the body.

Assisting the Physical Body:

Everything communicates, and the physical body is no different. You just have to learn to listen to what your body is saying. The body is so in tune with its surroundings that it even listens to our thoughts. Your body knows when feel like you hate it. Your body knows when you are happy. Your body knows when you are not paying attention to it.

Assist your physical body by communicating love and accepting it as the way it is. Expand your thoughts and beliefs regarding your body and realize how powerful it is. You can ask for headaches to lighten. You can say "hey, that hurts" and ask for easement in physical pain. At first it may not listen right away... the physical body has been ignored for quite some time. Trust has to be established in the relationship with your body; trust that you will take care of it on a conscious level.

Work with your body, and work with your thoughts about your body. Your relationship will surely change. We are not the person that looks back at us in a mirror. Each body is unique because each experience is unique.

Remember that you chose this body, you chose this experience. And you are the only one who can get okay with the choices you make. If you're having a hard time accepting your body for what it is, ask yourself why you are having such a hard time. What story are you telling yourself about your body? What story do you believe? And can you believe something new about yourself?

I am Not my Thoughts:

The human mind is a powerful thing: it can believe anything it wants to. We learn new things every day, and each new piece of the puzzle affects all the thoughts we have ever had, and will ever have. When we were designing this game we call life as a human being, we created the Ego as part of the experience we wanted to play out.

We wanted, as a collective soul body, to experience duality and survival. We wanted the mind to have contradictory thoughts to our feelings. We wanted the fight and we wanted the surrender. What thoughts are running around in your head all day? Do you like the thoughts you are having? Why do you think the way you do?

Listen to your ego, listen to your thoughts, and see just how ridiculous they are. You can say when enough is enough. You can put your mental foot down and say you want to come from love and peace from now on; love and peace for yourself and your experience. When we are trying to wake up, the ego's job is to get us off track. When we want to start loving our bodies and start doing more things for ourselves, the ego's job is to tell us we are wrong and selfish and that we should just go sit on the couch and binge-watch television.

The ego is the little voice that instills doubt. Our job is to come from faith, our true feelings within, and know what everything we do is perfect, that we are perfect, and this is just an amazing experience we are having as souls experiencing the human body for a short amount of time.

In regards to the awakening process and the changes in collective consciousness, the ego can evolve into what we refer to as a spiritual ego. When someone changes their lifestyle, adapting a specific way they want to live their lives, they can begin to believe their way is the best way and judge all others who do not see life as they do.

More specifically, when people adapt a more conscious lifestyle, whether that means not eating meat or using any sort of animal product, or juicing everything they eat, or doing yoga every morning, or living off the grid...all of these are wonderful ideas and perfect ways to experience life...but the problem is thinking that this is how everyone should be doing it and making others feel bad for not doing this way or that way.

People who consider their lives as being a more "spiritual" kind of lifestyle can fall into the same ego traps that we all fall into. I stopped eating meat a few years ago. At first I couldn't understand why other people still ate meat. I watched way too many documentaries on our global food production. I've been angry. I've judged people. And then I realized they judged me right back for not eating meat. So what if you eat meat and I don't? So what if I don't run a 5k every week? So what if I don't even run at all? The mental body does its job very well. It reminds us that we are not what we think. It reminds us that we are not what we think we do. Thoughts, opinions, are just a part of the game and we can choose to believe them or not.

Assisting the Mental Body:

When one starts to question their thoughts and starts to actively change their belief systems, the mental body can put up one hell of a fight. Its job is to re-direct us to what is safe, to what it knows. Change is scary to the ego. We want change all the time, and yet we are afraid of it, so rarely do we actively change unless it is forced upon us or the change has been a long time in the making.

Assist your mental body by understanding that it has a job to do. Appreciate your ego for keeping you safe and secure in the past.

It has done its job well.

But the past is past, and now is now. And it is okay to change your thoughts. It is okay to change your beliefs. Keep striving for change and don't take no for an answer, even from your own brain. Your thoughts served you at one point or another, so don't judge yourself for having a thought you now believe to be "wrong."

People change their minds all the time. You are allowed to do so. Maybe you hated your neighbor yesterday but you love him today. This moment is all that matters, so if you want to change how you think in this moment then that is perfectly okay.

Also, thoughts manifest in the physical body. So if you are having physical "problems" look at your thoughts behind them. Different areas of the body refer to different aspects of the mind. Dis-ease is created when thoughts are judged and suppressed. Get okay with your thoughts of the past, your worries of the future. Get okay with wanting to change or wanting to be a new person and experience life differently.

When the body hurts, it can mean that it is releasing thoughts and emotions that no longer serve. When you start to love your body, when you start to change your thoughts about your life, the old will come up to be released and dissolved from your reality. Continue to love and assist in any way that you can, and remember that nothing lasts forever.

I am Not my Emotions:

This is a feeling journey. However, we don't have to identify with

39

our emotions. We can just accept them as part of the programming, as part of the experience, and let them do what they need to do and move on after they are finished.

Emotions just want to be felt and experienced. Be aware of the feelings you have. You can choose to experience an emotion for what it is instead of letting the emotions run amok and run your world and your entire experience.

There is no such thing as an unhealthy emotion. People believe that if they suppress an undesirable emotion that they are doing something spiritual or beneficial to society. "I'm not angry because I'm not allowed to be angry because that is just not very spiritual," or "I shouldn't be grieving because I know I should be happy that my friend has moved on to a new experience," or whatever else you would like to say.

Today you are walking around and you are angry, or you are worried, or you are ashamed. Accept what you feel in this moment. Anger doesn't last forever, but if it does then that is a choice you've made to stay angry. Experience all range of emotion as just an experience; there is no right or wrong, no good or bad, emotions. All is perfect and meant to be.

Assisting the Emotional Body:

Crying is a difficult subject for many people. Some cultures even judge and criticize people for crying. Crying is simply allowing oneself to feel. Honor that need to feel; your emotional body wants to feel and suppressing that desire is not listening to, or assisting, your emotional body.

Do not suppress. Allow the emotion to arise and to become what it wants to in its expression. Understand that you are experiencing an emotion at that time. What are you attached to? Why are you feeling this way? Become aware of your emotions. Allow yourself to experience your emotions without judgment. All that matters is this moment, and what you are experiencing in this moment.

Denying an emotion can create dis-ease. As our thoughts can manifest in our physical bodies, so can our emotions. When we "bottle-up" our emotions we create this energetic vortex within our vessel. The longer we suppress feeling, often the worse that feeling gets. We keep adding to our feelings of anger, blame, guilt, betrayal, shame, loss, and fear until we can no longer contain our emotions and we lash out at ourselves and the world.

Honor your feelings. Honor your emotions. Sometimes you'll want to cry for no reason, and be okay with that. If you are angry, get angry. Go stomp your feet and scream and yell. When you're done move on to the next thing, no judgments. Also, allow other people their emotions as well. Honor their need to experience what they need to experience.

The Soul Body, or Higher Self:

The higher-self aspect is just another version of you. Our soul has experienced some form of life before and has chosen to experience it again this time, in the form of our life and journey on planet Earth. The soul is the viewer behind the curtain of life and beyond this vessel we call a human body.

Life is not so serious, only the human aspect makes it so. The soul sees all as growth, as a learning opportunity. Our higher selves

41

assist our journey, but can never do the journey for us. We have to make the choice to become more conscious in our actions. We have to choose to listen to our intuition or not. The soul may have set up the game, but we have the free will to play that game as we decide to.

The soul body reminds us that we already exist in a higher dimension. As a part of the higher dimensions, our souls impart knowledge and assist us on our journeys. We view the soul as being in control only because if the human aspect was in control it would mess up the grand plan simply by coming from a place of control.

The human controls how it wants to see the world, how things should happen, and the specifics of reality. The human wants the big screen television in the mansion with unlimited cash to buy whatever its ego desires at the time, out of fear of security, lack and control.

The higher self understands the needs of the ego, of the human aspect, and will provide everything it truly needs out of love. How that happens is not up to the human, because the human has control issues. The human doesn't see the unlimited possibilities and potentialities; it gets fixated on the one reality it wants, or thinks it needs, out of some form of fear.

Your higher-self is always communicating with you. How you access the information from that level of consciousness is just a matter of remembering how to do it. The heart is the seat of the soul. The human aspect operates from the head, or mental body.

Trust the feelings you feel from the heart, that is your soul trying to communicate something with you. If you feel something is wrong or off, it means that is probably not the path you should be taking at the moment. If your heart sings for joy at the thought of a new career then trust those feelings. Creativity inspires the soul and opens the heart for deeper communication with the universe. Do what makes you happy and practice trusting your own intuition and feelings.

Assisting the Soul Body:

On the soul level, we have accepted the program we call reality. The discord in life results from the human aspect failing to accept it as well. The human thinks it shouldn't have to accept the program, the reality, as it is. What is there to accept about what goes on in the matrix, the thoughts that roam in and out of our heads, and how we treat ourselves and each other every day?

Accept the parts of you that you wish to change, or hope would change. Accept and forgive yourself for how you've treated yourself throughout your life up until this point. Accept all the different aspects of yourself, whether you think you think they are bad or good. Acceptance is the ultimate goal for integration and unification of the body, mind and soul paradigm. If you don't accept yourself and your life the way it is, who will?

Remember that you have the power to change your reality. You can change your thoughts. You can allow your emotions to experience what they need to experience. You can appreciate the physical body you've chosen to experience everything life has to offer you on this particular journey. You'll get to play again when you're finished with this game. Stay in the moment and play with what your reality has to offer you now. Go with the flow and get okay with whatever you experience.

43

UNIFICATION OF SELF

"I'm afraid I can't explain myself, sir. Because I am not myself, you see?"

\- Lewis Carroll

It is quite fascinating that we are not our bodies, minds or emotions. We are simply aware of these bodies. We are a combination of all of these bodies, once separated and are now unifying as the planet and humanity ascend to a higher level of consciousness and understanding. When we unify the four bodies of consciousness we become the Light body.

Simply put, the Light body is the new paradigm, the new game we have agreed to play out on Earth as a collective soul body. Moving into 5th dimensional consciousness is all about dissolving the barriers and seeing each and every thing as One... including the planet, the solar system, the galaxy, the universe and Source Itself...and seeing ourselves as part of that whole magnificent dance. Unification of self is achieved through the ascension process as all aspects of yourself come together and are no longer separated as in the old paradigm of reality.

Our physical body, mental body, emotional body, and soul body have operated separately for millennium as per the agreement to experience everything as separate. Some souls still wish to participate in this game, and will go to other planets in the galaxy to continue learning at a 3rd dimensional level.

However, planet Earth is ascending and will complete its 5th dimensional integration by mid-March 2016, roughly. This means that planet Earth is no longer a 3rd dimensional planet that plays out density and survival (fear, lack, etc.). In order to continue playing on planet Earth in our physical forms, those who choose to stay must ascend to match the consciousness and energetic frequency of the planet. And the Light body is the vehicle for this ascension. The Light body is the new vessel for playing out an experience in a 5th dimensional world.

As a Light body, we view our experience as souls *inhabiting* a physical body *with* a mind built to *experience* thoughts and emotions. The merging of all aspects of self, of all experience of self, allows us to become a light being. We all have the power to unify our consciousness. It happens automatically in response to the frequencies being emitted from our reality but we can also consciously affect our consciousness by accepting the new paradigm of Oneness, instead of the old paradigm of separateness.

If you don't believe you have the power to unify your body, mind and soul together, just imagine the colors of the rainbow: they aren't actually separated, they blend together. Are there gaps in the rainbow? No there are not. Just like the rainbow, we are made up of many different aspects, but as one we form something beautiful and functional.

In order to assist your personal unification, let go of emotional attachments and expectations of what you think you should be experiencing. We are all ascending, in one form or another. We are all exactly where we are supposed to be on our journeys. It is your choice to come from neutrality and to get okay with what you are experiencing.

Assist your different aspects of consciousness and know that you are connected to every other thing in the universe as one being. Work with your body, your mind, and your soul by communicating, appreciating, and accepting everything they are and everything they have to offer during this time of personal and planetary change.

SYNCHRONICITY

"If you only knew the magnificence of the 3, 6 and 9, then you would have the key to the universe."
- Nikola Tesla

Synchronicities are communications with our higher selves. Until we learn to communicate directly with our souls we get messages in the form of number patterns, song lyrics, street signs, conversations with strangers, animals, tones and sounds, and many more. As souls, we setup reminders throughout our lives, with pre-programmed messages, before we came to Earth and began this little game.

Our souls, or higher selves, had certain goals they wanted to achieve this time around. We encoded interactions with people, places and things in order to experience specific things, to fulfill contracts, to bring up thoughts and emotions to let go of, and to ascend into higher dimensions of consciousness at the "right" time. Look and listen for all the signs and markers happening around your reality at this moment.

Notice what keeps coming up in your life, as repetition is meant to get your attention. Are you seeing a specific number pattern on the clock every time you look at one (11:11, 12:34, or 8:11)? Do you have a song lyric stuck in your head, repeating a word or phrase over and over again? Did someone start talking about something random you've been thinking of while riding the bus or train and they answer the question you've wanted an answer to? These are actually messages for you.

Intuition is a form of synchronicity. Being able to see the correlation within the events of your life as answers to your own life's questions on a conscious level is a way of understanding synchronicity. If you didn't like your job and you got laid off for "no reason," then perhaps your soul is trying to tell you something. We may not realize the little things in life add up, and that when something major like a job loss or losing a loved one can be considered a kind of "wake up call" from the soul to the human aspect.

Everything is a sign. Everything has a message, a purpose, and is here to assist us in expanding our consciousness in some fashion. You can ask for signs from your universe. You just have to pay attention to what the universe sends you as a response. It requires silent observation, a conscious awareness, and opening our hearts and minds to fully see and understand. Remember that this is your universe and that you have the power to ask for what you want.

Types of Messages:

-People: Interactions are encoded to bring up stuff for you. They are fulfilling a contract. Is someone making you angry, happy, or sad? Why or why not?

-Song lyrics: What are you trying to say to yourself? Also pay attention to when you change the words to a song, and you recognize that. The meaning is for you and you alone

-Numbers: Numbers have specific meanings that we have all

agreed to on a collective level. Find the interpretation that resonates within you. Numbers are also activations for us on our journey of awakening.

-<u>Animals</u>: Did you notice a pretty butterfly at the park? Are you seeing turtles everywhere you go (symbols, pictures, maybe even a real turtle in a place where you weren't expecting a turtle to be)? Each animal has its own meaning; you just have to figure out what it means for you. The internet is a helpful tool for deciphering messages.

-<u>Dialogue</u>: What pieces of a conversation are you catching around you? What conversations are you a part of? All dialogue has been designed by you, for you.

-<u>Tones</u>: What sounds are happening around you? Do you hear birds and don't see any? Do you hear wind-chimes without any wind present? Do you hear an alarm clock beeping inside your head? Listen and find the answer that feels right to you.

-<u>Road Signs/Shop Signs</u>: What *words* are you noticing around you? Do they keep repeating? Are you feeling sad and see something that cheers you up? Do you keep driving around on the "wrong" streets? Notice where you are in every moment.

-<u>Miscellaneous:</u> Trust your intuition. If you feel as if something is a message for you then it most likely is. This is your reality, this is your universe. Everything has been designed by you, for you.

Remember that the meaning behind our messages, our synchronicities, change in every new moment. What was true a moment ago can be a new truth in this new moment. And all meanings need to be our own metaphors. We can use others' interpretations to help find what resonates within us, but ultimately we can create our own markers. My list may be different for you, and vice versa.

<u>Number Meanings:</u>

The following interpretations associated with the main numbers 0-9 should be loosely interpreted. If a meaning for a particular number doesn't resonate with you, find an interpretation that does, including creating your own meanings for each number.

If you notice a number pattern that appears often in your reality, see what is going on in those moments. After all, numbers and the meanings behind them were pre-programed as messages from our higher-selves in a language that we would understand at the time we "download" the information along our journey. When numbers appear in sets of three or four (like 111 and 1111), it is meant to get your attention and to make you aware of your thoughts and/or what is going on in your reality at the time.

1's:
Monitor your thoughts carefully, and be sure to only think about what you want, not what you don't want. The number 111 is like the bright light of a camera flash, it means the universe has just taken a snapshot of your thoughts and is manifesting them into form. The 1111 number sequence if most often the first sequence that appears to people as they start to awaken.

2's:
Take a balanced approach to your thoughts. Everything will turn out for the best in the long-term. Do not put your energies into negativity and be aware that everything is being worked out for

the highest good of all.

3's:

The Ascended Masters are near you. They have responded to your prayers and wish to help and assist you in your current endeavors and with your Divine life purpose.

4's:

You have nothing to fear. All is as it should be, and all is well. Your angels are all around you, offering their support and love as you work towards your goals and aspirations. They are reminding you to call upon them for help whenever you need them.

5's:

A major life change is upon you. This change should not be viewed as being "positive" or "negative," since all change is but a natural part of life's flow. Ultimately change is always for the better as your higher-selves, angels and Ascended Masters have your best interest at heart.

6's:

Your thoughts are out of balance right now and are too focused on the material world. This means that you have been thinking too much on money and not your personal spiritual growth and family life. Focus on your personal spirituality in order to balance any issues in your life.

7's:

Keep up the good work! You have listened to Divine guidance and are now putting that wisdom to work in your life. You are on the right life path and know that your wishes are coming to fruition in your life as a result of your efforts and positive attitudes towards life. Expect miracles to occur in your life.

8's:

A phase of your life is about to end. This number sequence may mean you are winding up an emotional career, or relationship phase. It also means there is light at the end of the tunnel. Also, the number 8 brings about financial prosperity and abundance.

9's:

You have completed a big phase in your life and have learned a valuable lesson in the process. 9's also signify that this is the time for you to utilize your talents and serve your Divine life purpose at this time. Live your life in a positive and uplifting manner in order to teach others by example. You are a Light Worker and the angels ask you to live up to your full potential for the benefit of all.

0's:

A reminder that you are one with the universe. You are a powerful being with the ability to manifest all that you desire in your life. Also, it is a sign that a situation has come full circle.

PART TWO:

THE HOLOGRAM CALLED REALITY

THE PARADOX OF REALITY

"Everything we hear is an opinion, not fact. Everything we see is a perspective, not the truth."
- Marcus Aurelius

Physical reality has been constructed for the sole purpose of an experiment of consciousness and the accumulation of new experience under a certain paradigm. Reality is merely a holographic representation created from within our being and projected outward like a movie projection. Reality is simply a playground where one pretends to be human. This is a fixed reality for the human mind, and yet we are more than just human, so we can expand beyond the limits of the human box.

Reality is made up of a natural matrix, where there are general rules regarding structure and the codes of interaction and reactions, and then there is a superimposed matrix. The superimposed matrix is the matrix where everything is in reverse and gives a very polarized world, so that everything that is real is considered fake and everything that is fake is considered real. The superimposed world is a world of opposites. This matrix was designed and implemented into the basic coding of planet Earth as part of an agreement to experience a world of duality and polarity. We agreed to have this experience. And this agreement is coming to an end, at least on this planet. Each matrix has their own set of rules and experiences to play out.

The natural matrix of the world is an expansive matrix; it is connected to all other matrixes across the galaxy. Whether we are following the rules of a natural matrix or superimposed matrix, all a matrix is really designed for is to create a similarity in the sense of the projection of the planet: everyone would see everything the same way.

Each individual may have a different interpretation for what they see and a different way of how they view the reality around them, but if there is a tree in a park then we are all seeing a tree in a park. We may have different ways of seeing this tree but we are all seeing a tree, and the ground around it, and so on and so forth. That is what a matrix does: it gives us a basic operating system within it so that we can have a playground where we can consistently play together under the same set of rules. If one person saw a tree and another person saw a rock, conversation and interaction with that one object would be confusing and unnecessary.

However, since everyone is an individualized soul with their own aspects of self, each experience of the world is unique. We may all see a tree in a collective area, but we don't all see entire color spectrum, or light spectrum. We don't all experience sounds to the same degree. We don't all feel the same way in response to environmental stimuli.

The paradox of reality is that, while we've agreed to certain rules in order to live and interact with each other in a non-confusing manner, we also have our own individual hologram in which we operate from. Most of the time, the people around you cannot see what is in your hologram. Sometimes you can see something that no one else can. The skies change, colors change, and it all depends on what energetic frequency you are operating from. You can even pull people into your energy field and show them what you see. I didn't know I could see prana floating about in the world until my partner showed me how.

Many people live their whole lives by the rules of the game, never experiencing outside the confines of the boxed matrix. We don't even know all the rules of the game until after we've left the game. That is how our souls wanted it, and that is what we agreed to. While there are rules to the game, some people discover how to bend those rules at one point or another.

Realities shift as energy shifts. Walls breathe and objects move out of the corner of our eyes. We tell ourselves that it isn't real, but it is. Objects are not as permanent as we think they are. They constantly disassemble and restructure themselves, faster than the human processor can process and interpret. The human mind filters out a lot of stuff; if it isn't a part of the game it knows so much about then it just can't be real.

Decide what reality is true for you. Do you believe everything is as you've been told? We hold our hologram in place with our thoughts, our mind. Break down those thoughts and accept a new hologram as a new experience.

Projected Reality:
The hologram is constantly being upgraded and is constantly shifting. We change our hologram every time we move locations, every time we think a new thought, and every time we blink our eyes. A new version of the hologram resets with every new piece of information we acquire and every time we change our beliefs about something in our world. We create everyone and everything in our reality. We pre-programmed to forget who we really are and why we are really here when we started playing our new reality. And we pre-programmed when we'd start to remember this game.

57

The real world is not what we can see. We only see the hologram; the way our mind wants us to see it in order to prove its own point of view. The real world is so much more than what we can see, it is more than we can even imagine…and yet we believe what we see because that is safe and that is what we think we know. When we can know so much more, when we can be so much more, then what our mind tells us is "real" isn't as real as we once knew.

Reality is fluid. Often our expected reality is different than our actual, or perceived, reality. The human expects the world to work a certain way and when it doesn't it writes off the experience as a malfunction of programming. Everyone is right in their own reality. We are all in our own world and we are all experiencing our own timelines. We don't have to agree on anything because technically we are not in the same world. Conflict arises when we try to agree on things. Accept that we, as humans, don't have to agree on anything.

We agreed to all the matrix veils, yes. But we don't have to be a victim to them anymore. The veils are inside of us, and they are lifting as we are ready for them to do so. Reaffirming or reinforcing a certain thought or belief about yourself and the world around you only keeps one inside a limited hologram. When looking at a photograph of a person from two years ago, realize that that person technically doesn't exist anymore. Everyone has a role to play, and everyone's role can change in any moment.

The Scientific Approach:
What the human sees with its eyes is not real. The light from an object actually falls on our retina in a two-dimensional fashion. We live in a three-dimensional world.

Therefore, our brain has to take the best guess and convert that imagine into a three-dimensional form. All that we see in our world is just an approximated image produced by the human brain, which is influenced by thought (expectations, attachments and judgments) and our emotions (feelings about how the world should work). The visual sense might be the most powerful sense that we have as humans, but it can still trick us into believing what is not real. When adding the auditory sense to what humans can physically see, conflict can arise when what we see and what we hear fail to match up.

If you have ever tried to watch someone speak without sound, as in trying to lip read or by watching a silent movie, the brain can create its own version of events with the information it can gather. People with more in-tune senses can have a harder time distinguishing and experiencing the senses due to overstimulation, creating a form of reality that is gathered from the information they can pick out from the world.

Additionally, quantum physics continues to shed more and more light on the topic of reality by proving more and more that it is not as we think it is. According to a well-known theory in quantum physics, a particle's behavior changes depending on whether there is an observer or not. It basically suggests that reality doesn't exist unless you are looking at it. This theory is known as the "delayed-choice" experiment, or "quantum eraser," and it can be considered a modified version of the double slit experiment.

In order to understand the delayed choice experiment, we first have to understand the quantum double-slit experiment. In this experiment, tiny bits of matter (photons, electrons) were shot towards a screen that had two slits in it. On the other side of the screen, a high tech video camera recorded where each piece of matter landed. When scientists closed one slit, the camera showed one kind of pattern.

But when both slits were opened, an interference pattern emerged and the particles began to act like waves. This means that each particle individually went through both slits at the same time and interfered with itself. The single piece of matter became a "wave" of potentials, expressing itself in the form of multiple possibilities, and this is why the interference pattern emerged.

As for the delayed choice experiment, scientists observed a different phenomenon when a human tried to further measure the double-slit experiment. They found that when an observer decided to measure which slit the piece of matter went through, the wave of potential paths collapsed back into one single path. It was as if the particles knew they were being watched.

The delayed choice experiment has shown that an observer has some sort of effect on a particles' behavior. What does this conclude about the nature of reality? That humans influence their reality with thought. Particles are simply a form of energy, and energy can be manipulated in many different ways.

Another theory that questions the validity of existence is the concept of quantum entanglement which suggests that two objects (electrons) created together are "entangled," which means that if you send one object to the other side of the universe, and do something to one of them (like spin it), the other will act in the same manner instantaneously. Either information is traveling faster than the speed of light, or the vast distance we perceive between two objects doesn't actually exist.

RULES OF THE GAME

"Life is and will ever remain an equation incapable of solution, but it contains certain known factors."
- Nikola Tesla

We chose to play this game of life. We wanted a challenge, and we knew we could handle it. We just didn't realize how well we designed the game in the first place. With all the 3rd dimensional density, the polarity, and the duality, most of us never get around to remembering the divine part of our experience. We trudged head first into a game where we would make money, get an education, get a job, have a family, and worked until we were too old and left the Earth.

Why are there billions of people on the planet at this time? Why are we living longer lives in our human vessels? Because the old 3D game has changed and the old rules of aging no longer apply (unless you believe they do; remember the power of the mind). We are not our vessels. We wanted the experience of physical breakdown as a parameter of the old game. The vessels still on the planet are going through a shift in order to live in the higher dimensions. We chose to jump on this planet at this time in order to experience this physical ascension.

Although the game has changed and will continue to change, many people are still playing the old version of the software without any of the updates. As souls we put the human mind in charge to keep us powerless during the game while we were asleep.

The whole world out there was created so we would lose our power and subsequently remember it. It is because of this remembering that we agreed to give up our power in the first place.

We wanted the remembering experience. Each time we listen to the human mind, the ego, we agree to give up our power in that moment. The ebb and flow of the human mind/heart paradigm is the essence of the game. When you realize that you can choose to come from your heart instead of your head, you start to reprogram your reality by updating the holographic program.

We have all gone into agreement, on a soul level and on a human level, with our experience here on Earth. What we see, in many ways, is an out-picturing of a creation that someone thought and we have gone into agreement with. This is what you see when you go to the store, when you turn on the television, or sign onto a computer. We are always co-creating our reality.

If someone tears down a mall, someone else's thought, and puts up their own store, their own thought, everyone who is destined to come in contact with that store has agreed to that change in the hologram. But the matrix can be collapsed intentionally when you understand that it was born out of the need to control. The rules of the game can bend and break. When the structure of control collapses, the hologram becomes more malleable and flexible to the winds of change.

We made the rules of the game, the universe, and we can change those rules to fit our individual experiences. Your universe responds to the energetic vibration you are creating. What you send out, you get in return.

Thoughts and beliefs are powerful things. Words are powerful. The only true way to play the game is to figure out the rules; the rules are only energy after all. The rules are in place to give a certain kind of human experience, and that experience continues to diversify and expand with every new soul that comes to play on the planet. You programmed your reality. You just have to figure out how your program works, and then you can rewrite it.

When the Game Ends:

The game of life is not a game in the sense that there is a winner, or a way to win the game. There are no winners because there is no way to lose the game. The point is to experience as much as one signed up for in order to add to the unified field of Source consciousness, or the brain/parent of this entire operation we call the human experience.

We all derive from Source, and as a part of Source we are actually Source itself, as an aspect. The human fears what will happen when it loses the game, i.e. dies at the end. The soul doesn't fear the programming: it knows the program does what it is meant to do, and it knows that it is eternal.

The soul has a space that it holds itself in. In checking out, the human aspect looks at the physical death as something very traumatic. In reality, at the soul level, it is like parking your car, leaving it at the rental car agency, and deciding which car you want to take for a test drive next. Each time a soul takes on a physical form, it takes it as just another vessel in which to experience life from.

The vessel is simply a mode of transportation in which a soul gets into the experiential realm that we are in right now. When the soul leaves the body, it basically goes into a state where it waits to take on another form. There might be a review period in which it goes over its previous life, without judgment, and chooses how it wants to play next time. Our soul will continue to come onto this planet until it is finished with this evolutionary cycle, or until it achieves enlightenment, where it will no longer incarnate in this realm and go onto a new experience somewhere else in the universe.

Humans have a fascination with immortality and becoming immortal in their lifetimes. The human aspect thinks it needs other people to remember it in order for our lives to mean something. We are, in fact, already immortal. Earth is just a game, a program designed (by us) to play and learn from. And it should be a fun game, for we are its creators.

We can create the world we want to live in; we've designed all that we see already. We set all of this into motion before we were even born in order to learn. And we refine the program as we go along through life, if we choose to do so. The beauty of free will and choice allows for many different experiences at many different times. When we are done playing with one toy, with one experience, we go find a new one to play with until there are no more toys left in this toy box.

The Universal Box Conundrum:

If all there that exists is this moment, and there were no other moments before this one, how would you define yourself? How could you define yourself? Definitions only confine our existence to a box of labels. We are more than the proverbial box. Our limitless potential as divine beings cannot be confined to a finite contraption such as a box. We are the stars, the sun, the universe, the air; everything. When we define ourselves, we limit ourselves. And we are done with limits.

However, if you were to confine yourself to a box, as the human aspect needs to in order to bring meaning and purpose to life and its existence, what kind of box would you rather be in, in this moment? Would you rather be in a box of ugliness, failure, and contempt? Or would you rather be in a box of love, respect, and beauty?

It is your choice how to define, or see, yourself and your life. You are the only one who truly understands you. Everyone else sees you as they see themselves, because they don't know what you are thinking, or know of your life experiences, or the dreams you dream every day. That is all on you, for you, to express and truly know as yourself.

We make our own boxes. We put ourselves in those boxes. We keep putting one box into another box, and that box into another box, until all aspects of ourselves are boxed up. And then we keep ourselves in that box. The human aspect thinks boxes are safe, but a cardboard box gets wet in the rain. What story is keeping you in a box? Which story frees you?

The human mind is a computer: reprogram it. Where are your limits? What do you believe you can and cannot do? Why not? Look at your automatic programs, see where you have limited yourself, and see what you have gone into agreement in regards to the limits in your life.

The phrase "thinking outside the box" actually forces us into a different kind of boxed thinking. Boxed thinking is of the old paradigm. There is no box (like there is no spoon)! Thinking outside the box implies that a box exists and that you have already put yourself in that box. The human mind, in all its power, created those boxes and put us in them.

All the labels, all the definitions, and all the egoic standards of who we thought we should be, are not who we truly are. We are much more and much simpler than all the labels: we are love, plain and simple, yet powerful and all consuming. You have the power to choose a box-free life. You have the power to remain in the box too. It is an individual's choice; just remember that you have that choice.

THE ILLUSION OF TIME

Alice: "How long is forever?"
White Rabbit: "Sometimes, just one second."
- Lewis Carroll

The human aspect believes time is linear, because that is how time was initially programmed in this matrix, and also because the human has been conditioned to see time as behaving as such. Yesterday progresses into today, and today progresses into tomorrow. We see the world in sequences. On a universal scale, time is cyclical, with one Age progressing into the next until it completes a cycle and starts over again.

Reality, on the other hand, is both linear and non-linear, and it can be both at the same time. Our human minds can think of this moment and a past moment and a future moment all at once. Although time appears to function in a particular fashion, it is ultimately an illusion. Everything happens in one moment, and the illusion is time, or the separation of that moment into segments. Time doesn't go from point A to point B in a straight line, from left to right. Instead, time goes up and down as it expands vertically, or up and down from one point. Time consists of layers stacked on top of one another with just enough space between to appear as separated. Human life is just one dot on a map, and that map fans out upwards, downwards, sideways, forwards, and backwards in all directions. We experience all time at once and at once all time.

Everyone's reality is different. Imagine the complexity of that

67

statement: the amount of overlap in realities and the number of people you never cross paths with in a lifetime, and even the number of people you do cross paths with throughout the days, months and years of a life.

There are billions of people on planet Earth, and there are billions of realities co-existing and co-creating at the same "time." Because of free will, every direction of choice that differs from your soul's plan or central life purpose creates another parallel timeline in which you play out that choice. When one becomes more in alignment with their purpose, the more timelines and parallel realities collapse until they are fully operating from one experiential timeline. As humanity ascends, and as the planet ascends, timelines are collapsing without any effort. We no longer need an infinite infinity of timelines in order to experience the human life out on planet Earth in the 4th and 5th dimensions.

As we discussed previously, there are multiple "yous" that are operating on all levels of dimensions, working simultaneously. The twelve versions of you on this planet may be playing out lives in different time periods and locations. While this aspect of you is living life in the 21st century, another aspect of yourself could be playing as a peasant in medieval times or as a gladiator in ancient Rome. We get glimpses of our alternate lives in dreams, déjà vu, and flashbacks. Déjà vu is ultimately a glitch in the human holographic program. It is supposed to make one question their perceived reality. We can jump timelines or step into other parallels for a moment. We can be experiencing a new timeline with overlapping experience with an old timeline. Pay attention to the glitches in your reality's programming. Parallels merge, timelines collapse, and we get a glimpse into the truly fascinating function of time.

Imagination and Memories:

In the moment, you create only the next moment. We create what we need for our journey one step at a time. Timelines are fluid and a form of creativity on our part. Our imagination stems from a vast pool of memories from everywhere we have ever been, from this world and many other worlds across eons of time. Nothing that we can imagine is illusion; images are remembrances from past experiences and "future" experiences, or experiences that happened in a timeline occurring centuries from now.

Our past is only a memory. When we step out of that frequency, that reality dissolves away. The human mind reconstructs memory from the frequency it is currently operating from, meaning that a memory is never the same as the last time one remembers it, and definitely not the same as the original memory.

We don't see things as they are, but as the way we perceive them to be. The human mind is influenced by thoughts and emotions about a subject, and all of our memories are just a thought of a thought. We create attachments to the past, and in doing so miss out on the present moment. It is becoming harder and harder to live in the past as we ascend and let go of our attachments and judgments about our lives. In the 5th dimension, memories will be there, but our attachments to them will not.

Memories are ultimately located in a different dimension. Memories can leave us and memories can be retrieved when one needs them. The human aspect obtains many keepsakes and pictures during its lifetime in an attempt to hold onto its memories. The human fears losing something, so it obsesses over the past and fears the future loss of its memories, its keepsakes.

Memories are simply the remembering of the last time one thought about an event, never about the event itself. We change the past all the time by remembering a time when we last remembered a time about an event that happened. Events happen one way and we can remember them happening an entirely different way.

The past is not set in stone, nor is the future. We can live our entire lifetimes in the imagination alone. Add infinite timelines, multiple dimensions, parallel universes and ever-changing frequencies to the mix and we get an experience rich in possibilities. We just perceive our own personal piece of the infinite every time we live a new experience.

Our thoughts influence our perception of time: how we see our past, how we imagine our future. And each new thought alters those perceptions. We are never the same person as we were a moment ago, and this is one of the hardest things to understand. Although cell renewal rates differ across the body, depending on the organ or tissue system, our bodies will have entirely regenerated every cell in a roughly seven year timespan. That means we are literally new people every time our cells die and new ones are created.

Future thoughts, otherwise known as worrying, don't always need to happen in our perceived timeline. Sometimes we just play with timelines to discover what we want and don't want in our current reality. We have the power to manifest these future thoughts through our deepest desires. The energy flows where we intend it to go. If you don't like your thoughts about your past or your future, you can change them. We like to put ourselves into little time boxes and experience time in a certain way. Let go of the comparisons of time (past, future, present) and try not to measure time. How much time can you actually see throughout the day, every day?

Time Travel:

We do not exist in time. We exist in a space, and sometimes not even that. We exist in a moment, an experience. Teleportation and time travel already exist, just not in the way we thought it did. We are already time travelers; we jump timelines all the time, and we can choose to do so consciously.

Remember that time is not linear but more vertical; we literally jump up or down into new timelines, into new experiences of time. We can jump to a point in our life's timeline that would have taken us years to get to the "traditional" way by becoming conscious of our reality and by honoring our journey in every moment. Physical interaction with our realities is required in order to "jump" these massive amounts of "time."

Time exists in every moment and in every direction. The place you are physically occupying has layers of other worlds and other times that are only separated by vibrational frequency. Many people have gotten glimpses and have interacted with these other worlds and other times. Seeing ghostly apparitions is a form of time traveling; one person has simply entered the realm of another.

Many people interact with beings from another dimension or

time period and don't even know it, mainly because they don't know this kind of thing happens and also because the human mind would block out the information and label it under the fear category.

Human beings exist on a limited range of vibrational frequency. Certain animals, like the common house cat, operate from a wider range of frequency and can experience things beyond the perception of the human mind. Cats often see ghosts and beings from other dimensions on a regular basis. The human thinks the cat is just staring at the wall, when in fact the cat knows something the human doesn't.

Like a band of frequency on a radio, the human frequency can be dialed into by other beings that operate in a different band of frequency and energy; this is how we get visitors from the galaxy to planet Earth and sometimes people can pick up on that. As humanity expands its energetic abilities and raises its vibrational frequency as it ascends, more and more access to the energetic frequencies beyond our range will become available. What exactly is out there for humanity to discover and experience through our many senses? Only time will tell.

WHAT DIMENSION AM I IN?

"A mind that is stretch by new experiences can never go back to its old dimensions."
- Oliver Wendell Holmes

A dimension is just a state of vibrational frequency. Everything is in a certain dimension. Your personal vibrational frequency dictates which dimension you are in. Those who operate from a lower range of vibrational frequency exist in the lower dimensions.

As we raise our frequency we move from one dimension into the next; on Earth we all start in the 3rd dimension. Some people exist in the 4th dimension and some exist in the 5th dimension, or higher. Although we are all operating from the general matrix, where there are rules that govern how we interact with one another, we often see and experience differently depending on what dimension we are in.

Realities are different in different dimensions; pancakes can taste better one day and not the next, we can notice more red-colored cars while driving and then all blue-colored cars in the next blink of an eye, and we can feel freezing cold in the sunshine and burning hot in the rain, all because of vibrational frequency.

As our journeys can span the course of time, spawning infinite parallels and alternate realities, we also inhabit all dimensions at once. Our souls, or higher-self aspects, are named as such because they, or us, exist in a higher dimension; they have already ascended the 3rd, 4th and 5th dimensions and are now acting as guides on our journeys of lower dimensional experiences. When people talk about guardian angels and angel guides, those are often aspects of ourselves from another dimension that have agreed to assist us at a specified "time" along our journey.

Similarly, humans operating from two different dimensions can appear invisible to one another. This is why we can experience phenomenon such as ghosts, extraterrestrials, and Big Foot, among others. Those beings exist in a different dimension, or a different vibrational frequency, than we do. We can tap into those frequencies, travel into those dimensions, and experience an interaction with those beings for the moment.

The human mind sees what is wants to and filters out a lot of extraneous stuff that it just can't be bothered with. The human programming is limited from a dimensional aspect, but once it is opened to the possibilities of other realities, dimensions, realms, and frequency, it can comprehend and "see" more of what actually exists in our realities. In order to see and understand more of what happens in the hologram, the human mind needs to expand in order to expand its possibilities.

So how do we move from one vibrational frequency to the next? First of all, it happens naturally during the course of human and planetary ascension. But those who are aware of the dimensions only need to make the conscious choice to raise their vibrational frequency, and thus ascend, on their own.

Whatever frequency one operates from is what gets transmitted, or projected, into their reality. Are you coming from love or are you coming from fear? Fear is a lower dimensional experience, while love is a higher dimensional experience. Our realities are based the energy we project; the hologram changes to the changes we make from our thoughts, beliefs and actions throughout our lives.

If you want to have a reality full of love, you must come from, or project, the energy of love. When you send out enough love, it comes back to you, and that cycle of energy continues and grows, as long as you continue to feed love, gratitude and appreciation back into your reality. We receive what we give, as per the laws of universal energy exchange.

Overall, there are at least twelve dimensions the soul body can experience from. What we have experienced as life on planet Earth for the past millennium is considered the 3rd dimension: a paradigm of duality, survival, and fear-based reactions. The 4th dimension introduces the experience of polarity. Polarity takes the concept of duality further by focusing on the extremes: beings in the 4th dimension experience complete loss, maximum pain, blinding anger, and so on. The 4th dimension is like a purgatory between the lower 3rd dimensional realm and the higher 5th dimensional realm.

The human heart, or the seat of the soul, operates from the 5th dimension. In the 5th dimension, experiences are played out as neutral; interactions between beings are more understanding as they operate from the premise that everything happens for a reason and that we are all fulfilling contracts. Beings exist in a frequency of love in the 5th dimension, and there is no need to experience fear or the survival mode as in the lower dimensions.

Beyond the 5th dimension, the soul experiences life in various states of form and non-form. Dragons are believed to come from the 7th dimension, although choose to exist in the 4th dimension because they can express their density, or form, in this dimension (this is what we consider the stereotypical dragon form). 12th dimensional beings have completed their journeys of experience and can choose to dissolve back into Source if they are not assisting other souls at the lower levels of dimensions.

There are many interpretations of the different dimensions, and although we know some things, we are not meant to know all as humans in this lifetime. As souls, we know all of this information already and will remember it after we leave this human vessel.

Multi-Dimensionality:

Again, we exist in multiple dimensions at one time. And because we exist in multiple dimensions, we can experience life multi-dimensionally. We can look at the moon and see more than one because of the level of frequency we inhabit allows us to do so.

We can experience the emotions of anger, sadness and shame while coming from a place of love and understanding, allowing those emotions to play out their role without judgment.

Where else can you live multiple lives, multiple experiences, at once? The universe is a playground in which one individual aspect of Source can accomplish so much in just one lifetime. When the soul works multi-dimensionally, it makes progress on its journey in an infinite manner.

Different versions of you exist in each dimension and frequency.

The human aspect will grieve the loss of the lower realms because humans want to grieve; honor that need to grieve, and honor the need to cry. Our higher selves are often happy with its experiences, and we can feel both emotions at the same time. There is nothing wrong with you when this happens! This is the multi-dimensional aspect of ourselves: we can experience many different things at once.

As higher dimensional beings, we can cry one moment, laugh the next, and go scream and yell at the top of our lungs right after. We are living multiple lives at once, and as we become more aware of our energetic vibrations, we often can move between those lives and all those experiences in rapid-fire succession.

Remember that the goal of life is to experience, and working multi-dimensionally adds to the infinite amount of knowledge our souls gather in just one lifetime.

So who will you choose to be? What path will you walk? Which side will you choose when you get to a fork in the road? Multi-dimensionality is a choice. There is only now, so which parallel existence do you want to experience at this moment? Honor the space you are in before moving onto a new space. Get okay with your experience and ask for a new one.

The lower realms never leave us, as we inhabit all dimensions at once. We just integrate them into our story and move on. Become mindful of the alternatives in your reality. Pick a new reality in the moment if you don't like the one you are in. It takes a lot of choice and action to change one's energy and the dimension they inhabit, but if you stick with it, you can create amazing things in your many realities.

Realms, Rifts and Portals:

Realms are another word for dimensions, but we see them as physical planes of existence instead of a more ethereal existence, like the fields where unicorns roam and the little door at the end of the rainbow where leprechauns live. While realms express themselves through a dimension, they are not necessarily from that dimensional consciousness.

Dragons usually emanate from the 4th dimension in order to experience 4th dimensional density but they are not 4th dimensional beings. Angels often come from the 6th dimension but are not necessarily 6th dimensional beings. The angelic, dragon, elemental, magical, fairy, monster, and mermaid realms (among many others) are all present in our reality at all times: in order to experience these realms we have to match their vibrational frequency in any particular moment.

There are frequencies and portals that open from each realm at different times for upgrades and assisting planet Earth in this time of ascension. These beings only assist us on our journey, and only the human aspect believes they could harm us in any way.

Another way to look at realms is as another plane of existence not typically from our realm of humanity. These realms exist on another plane because time and space are not what we think they are. Realms open and close their access to this plane of existence at different times but we can consciously choose to access these realms with practice.

Rifts are portals, or gateways, into the other realms. Have you ever noticed a car rift on a highway? I've taken many long-distance road trips across the United States and there can be long stretches of road where there is nothing around you, including other drivers, for hundreds of miles, and then suddenly you can find yourself being overtaken by a flood of other drivers in the middle of nowhere. I call these car rifts and they are designed to test your patience while driving.

Realms can be opened by anyone; all we have to do is ask, pay attention, and expect the new to come forth. The human mind will do everything in its power (which is substantial) to keep you distracted. You can go all day and complain when your day wasn't magical enough, or get discouraged that you didn't see anything new. Were you looking? Are you appreciative for what you do experience in every moment? Gratitude calls the energy of abundance to you. Gratitude brings forth more opportunities, new experiences, and easement of experiences you don't want to experience any longer.

The gifting realm does exist; you just have to open it up yourself in order to receive. You can't receive a gift if you can't accept it. Sit with the discomfort of having to accept money from other people if you usually turn down their offer. If you are constantly turning gifts away, your universe stops sending them to you. Become mindful of your actions and consciously choose to walk into portals and activate energetic vortexes to the other realms. You just might like the experience that is waiting for you when you do.

THE DREAMWORLD

"Dreams are true while they last, and do we not live in dreams?"
- Alfred, Lord Tennyson

Although many of the other dimensions and realms are not as readily available, we all utilize at least one other dimension in our lives, and that is what we consider the dream world. As part of the agreement and programming when we began this game, the human aspect agreed to sleep at certain times in order for the soul aspect to play out certain experiences.

If the human aspect was awake all the time, the human ego would only allow the experiences it thought were worthy enough to have. The soul aspect sets up an experience and lets the course of events happen naturally. In the dream state, the barriers are removed, the perceived limits are removed, and there are no rules. The soul utilizes the dream state in order to play out timelines, parallels, and pieces of old stories so we don't have to in an awakened state. The dream world is a realm of super play time.

The dream world is a particular realm that humans can utilize to access the many layers of multiple dimensions in order to interact with and learn from other aspects of ourselves, other beings, and other states of form and formlessness. As humanity is ascending, the dream state is becoming more and more of a tool to clear timelines from our energetic fields.

As we collapse timelines and parallels by consciously choosing to do so, our souls are doing the same through the dream state. Dreams are intricate plays of the different aspects of ourselves visualizing and experiencing all other existences we have contracts with to complete. And we work very hard in those dreams. We live many lives in our dreams; all of which is for the expansion of knowledge and growth with that infinite experience.

Dreams are dimensions in and of themselves. A lot happens in this dimension, and most of the time the human aspect cannot remember what happens while it sleeps. Rest assured (pun intended) that you accomplish a lot when you sleep whether you are aware of it or not, and it is all for the highest good and assistance for your ascension as divine beings.

We play in the dream state without all the constraints of the matrix and the veils of the human mind in order to work through multiple dimensions at one time. Just think of all the work you've done in your sleep in just one lifetime. The more work one does in the sleep state, the more one can focus on having a more conscious human experience.

For those who can remember their dreams, the meaning of your dreams is ultimately a personal quest. Dreams are not just parts and pieces of you, but as whole versions of yourself living lives simultaneously in a different dimension other than your own. We can access our other lives through our dreams, whether they are in this lifetime or across lifetimes past and future, and connect with those other versions of people and events. We can even share dreams with the people next to us in bed.

By utilizing the dream state, we can wake up in a new reality by having cleared a lot of old programming through the night (or whenever you sleep). Dream interpretations are personal because the dreams you have come from your personal frequency of experience. This is your life, and these are your dreams for a reason.

There are many books and websites devoted to the meaning of dreams, the symbols within dreams, and how to influence your dreams. While a particular dream may have meaning for you, it may not be what another person has interpreted from their personal experiences. If a meaning of a particular symbol doesn't resonate with you, then it is not a part of your personal truth.

Not all dreams have meanings and the meaning behind symbols can change. Dreams are not good or bad, that is just a human perception. Only the human aspect tries to find meaning in its dreams in order to attach an expectation and judgment onto them in order to feed its own version of the story. Just know that you are accomplishing many things when you sleep, and many contracts are coming to an end by utilizing the dream world.

VIBRATION AND FREQUENCY

"When you change your vibration, you change your hologram."
- Lisa Transcendence Brown

Reality is vibrational. There is a physical reality in every dimension; in every band of frequency. We are vibrational beings. We can bypass the feeling of time through our vibration: the higher we vibrate the less time affects us, i.e. time can appear to speed up, slow down, or even stop entirely. Time is a flow of energy, and since we are energetic beings, time can appear to expand and contract similar to our human breathing. In the present moment, you can create something in ten minutes that would have taken you months or years to complete. Time, as a vibrational energy, can appear to come to a halt when used as it was intended: an experience.

Vibrational frequencies can affect our physical, mental, and emotional bodies. Everything is a reflection of its energy and what band of frequency it inhabits. Pay attention to your vibration as you interact with other people, other creatures, and objects in your reality. The differences in vibration, frequency, and energy have all been designed to assist in our ascension. Although certain frequencies can make the physical body nauseous, instill doubt in the human mind, and stimulate the emotional body without reason, all is as it should be and all is of the highest good.

We no longer have to act as victims to frequency. These

vibrations from the universe bring upgrades to our four bodies of consciousness. Everything is technically ascension: all experience in all its forms. The human aspect may become uncomfortable with these upgrades, and judge what it is experiencing, but the universe only comes from love as only an expression of pure love.

As 3rd dimensional beings, humans operate from a low level of vibrational frequency. For the past millennium, before the end of 2012, humans mostly operated in a frequency below 175 Hz. As a reference point, the frequency of 528 Hz is the frequency of love and of 5th dimensional consciousness. Since December 21st, 2012, humanity has ascended steadily into the low 200s Hz as the planet has ascended through the 400s Hz. Those beings still on the planet after the planet fully ascends into 5th dimensional consciousness will be operating from a higher vibrational frequency ever known to the human experience before.

With all the upgrades occurring at this time, the raising of our vibrational frequency creates a range of discomfort, depending on your personal experiences. While we can consciously raise our vibration, and many humans are now operating above the 528 Hz frequency into the several thousands, every shift in vibration creates change.

In order to ascend into higher frequencies of consciousness, the lower frequencies have to drop away. Since humans have operated from the lower frequencies, creating attachments, expectations and judgments to its many experiences, those attachments have to drop away in order to "lighten" or enter the higher dimensions.

Density:

Density is a vibration that consists of dense material (thought, emotions, attachments, fear, anger, shame, blame, guilt, depression, judgments, etc.). In order to vibrate at higher frequencies, we need to release density, or our lower vibrational baggage in a sense. Remember that our goal is to become our Light bodies, with the key word being "light" here. Physical density is created from thoughts and emotions because thoughts and emotions are stored in the physical body.

You can tell how dense a person, place, or thing is by its characteristics. If it is raining outside a particular area, notice how long it rains. The longer it rains, the denser that geographical area is. Rain is cleansing; the planet assists in raising our vibration in any way that it can. When someone is walking down the street, you can tell how dense they are by the weight of their steps. And this has nothing to do with the weight or appearance of the individual. Even a 90-pound girl can walk around and shake the ground as if she were a 12,000-pound elephant, depending on how dense her reality is.

So what feels lighter to you: love, bliss and magic? Or, guilt, anger and sadness? Density is a feeling. We have the power to sense vibration and energy, so trust what you are feeling. Even colors carry their own vibrations. Dark clothing is denser. Bright colors are lighter. Walk around your local supermarket and sense the difference between two packages of food. An apple can feel lighter than a box of crackers. And organic apples can feel lighter than traditional apples. To affect your vibrational frequency, you have to become mindful of the differences in frequency and energy. Practice sensing between denser and lighter objects. With enough practice, one can become a master of energy, vibration, and frequency.

How to Raise your Vibrational Frequency:

We often don't give ourselves enough credit for what we can accomplish as human beings. We are such powerful creatures that we can intentionally affect the energy, vibration and frequency in our realities. The more one becomes conscious in this state, the more conscious they become in another state, such as the dream state, or vice versa. Opening up your heart by consciously coming from a state of love and gratitude in your daily actions and thoughts is one of the ways to ascend faster into the 5th dimension.

Our automatic programming can still operate from a lower frequency, so becoming mindful of one's programs can be helpful. If you always get mad at the checkout line at the grocery store because there is a long line, re-train your brain to think something different about your experience: express gratitude that there is at least one cashier available; offer to let someone with less items to go ahead of you out of respect for their time; and most importantly, tell yourself that you are waiting in that line for a reason and that it is okay. Once you get okay with a situation, you can ask your universe to get through the store faster next time.

Anything that makes you happy raises your vibrational frequency. Doing something that makes you smile or laugh is a conscious way to raise your vibration. Figure out what works best for you. I've found that smiling, even when I don't feel like smiling, improves the quality of day I am having. At first I had to force myself to turn the corners of my mouth upwards. Over time, it becomes easier and easier to just smile for no reason, and the more one smiles, the more smiles one gets in return. Surround yourself with people and things that make you happy, truly happy that is.

Do not compromise your happiness for the perception of another's. It is your responsibility to come from love, honor, and beauty, not as a result or byproduct of someone else's energy.

Additionally, become mindful of your surroundings. Stuck energy is vibrating at a lower frequency that energy that moves. Move the furniture around your house every so often. Get some new artwork and plants to lighten the place up. Move your work area around, and remember to move your physical body to get the energy flowing.

Plants and lots of light raise the vibration of a room the quickest. Color changes assist as well; balance darker tones with fresh pops of color to brighten the room. And anything that makes you feel peaceful assists in raising your vibration. I place crystals and little bonsai plants around my apartment. I would also like to get a water fountain so I can enjoy the sights and sounds of water cascading over rocks in my own private sanctuary.

If you don't have access to, or the ability to change your environment, all one has to do to ascend is simply go out in the sun every day. Light from the sun lightens our physical, mental, and emotional bodies. Simply look up into the sky and admire the clouds during the day and the stars at night. Connect with the earth, as the planet is in agreement with our soul bodies to assist in our ascension all the time. Humans who go out in nature often raise their frequency at a faster rate than those who do not. Honor what you feel you need for your journey. You can raise your vibration by sitting on the couch all the time; you just have to know what you are doing.

Traveling is also one of the fastest ways to activate and raise our vibrational frequency by going from dense locations to lighter locations. If you feel called to go on a certain vacation, or feel like you need to move to a new area, know that your soul has planned that travel with your highest good in mind.

I've driven from Denver to Phoenix many times in my life and although I always follow the same route, I ended up going off script on my last trip to get gas on a road I usually bypass. It didn't really bother me at the time, but it wasn't until after I got home that I realized why I made that detour; there was a certain vibrational frequency of the area that I needed to interact with in order to clear some old human stuff that was hanging on. Go with the flow of your universe, we may not understand why things happen, but everything works out in the end.

ENERGETIC FLOW

"If you want to find the secrets of the universe, think in terms of energy,
frequency and vibration."
- Nikola Tesla

If you don't believe in energy, or that you are an energetic being, just imagine how much energy it takes to maintain the holographic matrix of illusion and control. We are powerful beings, and we are amazing energetic creatures! Energy is universal; the same energy that makes up our beings also creates the stars in the sky, the leaves on a tree, a raindrop from a cloud, and a concrete wall.

Energy manifests in different forms but it is used in the same way as the building blocks of all reality. Let's work backwards for a moment: reality is what you see, hear, feel, taste, and smell, which is all interpreted by the human brain that forms thoughts and opinions about what it senses on a daily basis. Those thoughts are really just words, words with meaning attached to them, or words with intention: the intention of energy.

Energy created the coffee table in front of your couch. Energy created those pairs of shoes you use to explore the world around you. Energy shifts to who, what, where, when, why, and how it is needed.

We create everything and everyone in our reality through energy. The human body is a conduit for universal source energy, and if you follow the energy you give out, you will find the energy that your universe sends you in turn.

The heart emits a particular energy, while the head emits a different energy. We are affected in ways we don't realize as our perception, the human mind, influences how we see energy around us. The human aspect asks from a place of fear and lack, while the soul and heart asks from a place of love and abundance. When you are receiving a particular reality, notice what kind of energy you are coming from.

Our realities are simply an expression of the energy we view as our life. We are responsible first to our own energetic fields. Let others come from honor, love, and respect while you focus on your own energy. Energy can affect physical matter, including the human body.

What kind of thoughts are you having about yourself? What kind of energy are you sending your body?

Remember that the physical body of consciousness listens to the mental body of consciousness. If your thoughts are out of alignment with what you truly want your experience to be like, you will feel as if something is off about the other aspects of your life. Focus on what you do want, instead of what you don't want.

Intention:

Move your energy in the direction you want it to go. If you want to be a painter, then start painting. If you want to be a writer, then start writing. If you want to be an athlete, then start walking.

Set your intention for the day and focus on moving forward through the present moment. Be aware of your energy and maintain your own energetic fields. Are you avoiding something? Are you waiting for something else to happen before you can move on? If you are constantly waiting, then that is the energy you get from your universe in return.

Stuck energy doesn't flow properly. Try to actively work towards your goals, at least not by waiting for something to happen, or for a later time, in order to start a project. The soul body doesn't wait for someone else to fix all of its perceived problems, and it doesn't wait for someone to save it. Waiting keeps you in a cycle of waiting: waiting for gifts from the universe, waiting for abundance to enter your life, and waiting to jump forward on your journey without personal effort.

Energy is ultimately controllable through thought, or true intention. This means that if you truly believe that you can control and shape energy to suit your needs within your reality, then that is exactly what you can do. Anytime you "do" something, the energy in which you do it from is creating the reality that you get.

Sharing, instead of acting selfishly, creates unity again in your reality. Giving comes from a place of attachment and lack, when one person expects something in return for giving a gift or lending money. What energy are you feeding in your daily actions? We also eat according to vibration, so are you feeding an emotion or are you simply eating a piece of cake because you want that experience? Monitor your automatic programming and see where the intentions behind your actions come from, and thus, what energy you are emitting in any moment.

Money as an Extension of Energy:

Energy is focus. Energy is intention. The human aspect agreed to participate in this hologram of survival and lack by utilizing the experience of money as a form of exchange of goods. Money is just an extension of our personal energy. If we constrict our use of money, we are constricting ourselves. Lack creates an energetic cycle of lack.

If you think you only have one dollar left to your name, then that is what you have. If you think you are abundant with whatever amount you have, then you are abundant. Again, what energy are you feeding with your thoughts? What energy are you receiving in return? What if you saw everything as a sign of how abundant you are? When we change our perception of money, money changes to our perception of it.

Replace the words you use every day with "energy":

Money = Energy. Time = Energy. Thoughts = Energy.

Money, and how we experience it in our reality, is just a reflection of our energy. Time is also just a reflection of our thoughts. What do your thoughts say about your energy? We allow money to come to us in response to our energy, not the other way around. Identify what energy you are operating from at any given moment. Are you asking your universe for more money to come to you? Are you limiting yourself with money by not buying what you need to further your journey? How much do you think you are worth? Once you figure out the energy you are operating from, you can change how you want to interact with the energy in your reality.

LOVE vs FEAR

"Seeking love keeps you from the awareness that you already are it."
– Byron Katie

There are two forces in the world: love and fear. The human aspect has experienced fear for millennium, as per the programming of the superimposed matrix of duality and survival. Fear is held in the physical body as density and lightens as one ascends. Be the one to love you more than anyone else ever has, and you will transform that fear you've carried for so long in your reality to into the light of the fifth dimension and higher. While we are still playing out our contracts involving duality and survival, ascension becomes a duality of sorts: if you are not coming from love, then you are coming from fear.

The human aspect fears the program. Fear is an illusion. Fear is of the old paradigm; there is no way you can manifest the wrong thing, or a bad thing. Nothing outside of what the universe already has planned for us can happen. Imagine all the children who fear the monsters under their beds…we'd have a monster infestation if children could actually manifest their darkest fears. One cannot manifest something that isn't already supposed to happen for your highest good to further your soul's journey as an experience. The human becomes motivated by fear and reacts out of fear. If you believe that you are not allowed to progress beyond a certain point in your journey because you are unworthy, or fearful of the unknown, that is how the human mind controls its version of the journey. Fear prevents us from growth.

Ultimately, the human aspect is afraid of everything. It's scared of breaking the rules, and most of all fears the day you realize you are more than this empty shell in this hologram we call reality. How can it justify everything it has ever done out of fear of survival when there was no need to survive at all? We can appreciate the human aspect, the mind, for everything it has done for us. As we choose to grow and move beyond the perception and experience of fear, we outgrow certain beliefs and modalities of life.

Fear is a choice we make, so make it consciously from now on. Don't let your automatic programs and thoughts continue to run your world. There is fear, and then there is worrying that your fears will come true. Fears will continue to surface in new experiences, but you have the ultimate choice to let them control how you live your life. Ask yourself: "what's the worst that can happen?" Listen to all the thoughts that come up when you ask this question. Make a list of your answers, and then get okay with everything happening on that list. So what if that happens? How realistic are your fears anyway?

As fear is a choice, so is love. Love is an energetic frequency to express and maintain as a constant state of being. True love, the love of the soul and the universe, is unconditional. One of the goals of the human aspect is to remember that we are beings of pure love, and nothing less than such. If you don't love yourself and your reality at this moment, that is okay. You will. If you think your family never loved you, that is okay too. Many children are not taught how to love themselves, and you can't truly love someone else, as an aspect of yourself, until you love the "you" that is living this experience.

When we came to Earth, we agreed to participate in conditional love as an experience. The human aspect tends to love other people and other things only if they do something specific to earn that love. Unconditional love consists of loving everything as it is: no expectations, attachments, or judgments. Everyone is worthy of love. *You* are worthy of love. Love yourself first and expect others to love themselves before being able to love you.

Love is ultimately a choice. We can choose to love someone for who they are, or not. We can choose to love the animals in our lives, or not. We can choose to love ourselves, and we can choose to hate ourselves. Whatever you think, you are. If you are expressing the energy of love for your four bodies of consciousness, then your physical, mental, emotional, and soul bodies will show you love in return. If you are expressing disgust and hate for your body, then your body isn't going to feel that good. If you think your expressions of emotions are wrong, then your entire reality can feel wrong and unsupportive. Decide whether you want to continue playing in fear, or if you want to experience love in all aspects of your life.

The Language of Light:

The universe speaks, and we understand it through tones; as an energetic exchange. As humans, we interpret that communication with our universe as light and light codes. If we can utilize the sun to raise our vibrational frequency, then that means the sun is programmed to communicate with our four bodies of consciousness here on planet Earth to assist in our ascension.

One of the main goals of life is to accumulate more light, because light is the new currency of cellular function as humans ascend into light beings in the 5th dimension. The more light we hold, the more we can speak and act as light itself. We are the entire universe. Learn to communicate with it and the possibilities are limitless for the types of experiences we can have as we play on planet Earth.

Our language changes along the way as we grow from our experiences. When people can't find the words they need to communicate an idea with someone else, they are actually expanding their vocabulary at the time. Our words change depending on which dimension we are in. sometimes the switch between dimensions can take several days. Memories go in and out at this time as we acclimate to a new frequency of existence. Memories will come back, words will come back. It is as if the memories go out to the drycleaners and come back lighter, with the cords of attachment gone.

You can even change your words consciously in order to change your reality. Manifestation is just a cosmic word game. We can create love and abundance by sharing love and abundance within our reality. Manifestation is a human word, while materializing is a word the higher-aspect uses. We can change flu-like "symptoms" into "light upgrades" during the ascension process to assist our journey. Humans learn and the higher-self remembers. Humans help others on their journey, while the higher-self assists. Go beyond the perception of time and call forth the new into your reality with a change in vocabulary and belief system. You can change the way you view loss, sickness, and anger (among many other things) but only by changing your thoughts about those things. And thoughts are just words after all.

PARADIGM SHIFTS

"The way is not in the sky. The way is in the heart."
- Buddha

Paradigm shifts are simply changes that happen on a collective scale, whether the change is happening universally, galactically, planetary, or personally. We have collectively decided to ascend from 3rd dimensional consciousness to 5th dimensional consciousness on planet Earth.

Many souls will have the opportunity to opt out of this ascension process and either go to another planet to continue a 3D experience or to come back to earth as a higher dimensional being. Earth as we know it will be fully integrated into 5th dimensional consciousness by the end of March 2016 and will be unable to support most of the 3rd dimensional souls still on the planet. All souls have a choice to either ascend physically or leave the planet and continue their journey elsewhere. Overall, this process started 12/21/2012 with several upgrades and major shifts that have happened since that time.

One of the major universal changes that happened at the end of 2012 was that the universe entered the Age of Aquarius. With this change, the collective soul body made a new agreement for a new experience that would be different from the experiences in the Age of Pisces that we had been playing in for over two thousand years.

97

So yes, technically the world ended in 2012. We shifted into a new world with changes to our planetary structure and the structure of the entire universe. It's as if we tore down the old wooden rollercoaster of the last age and built a new steel coaster and upgraded all the tracks and cars for all souls to ride for the next two thousand years. With the many thousands of planets, galaxies and universes that exist, each planet, each galaxy, and the universe itself has its own programming and parameters for souls to play on. All of these layers of guidelines and possibilities allow for an expansive and entertaining experience across the cosmos.

Although the human aspect is affected by planetary changes here on Earth, there are things on going on a galactic level that don't necessary affect humanity's ascension but are going on nonetheless. The entire universe is ascending. Many 3rd dimensional planets are in the process of ascending or have already ascended, or transitioned, into the higher realms.

We as a soul body have collectively played out the 3rd dimensional duality, fear, and survival-based programming so well and for so long that it is time to move onto a new experience. There are a lot of 4th dimensional planets that utilize the experience of extreme polarity in order to get 3rd dimensional souls over the duality part of the game. And when souls are ready to move on, there are many 5th dimensional and higher planets to play on that allow more interactive gameplay.

In the 5th dimension, beings are highly in-tune with their natural abilities of creation, and can participate in any experience of their choosing. Overall the goal of the human right now on planet Earth is to ascend, and we ascend by changing our thinking, and changing our frequency in order to change our experiences.

We, not I:

When we become aware that our realities are interconnected with everyone and everything on the planet, and the entire universe, we start to understand unity consciousness. We are no longer perceived as individualized souls who have an individual experience that is separate from our fellow souls, but rather as a sort of Oneness.

We are one with the universe, and we are one with one another, and we are one with all beings. The animal kingdom has long been forgotten as just another aspect of ourselves, but this viewpoint is changing as humanity ascends and we become more conscious of our animal brothers and sisters. The way we interact with each other and the animals around us is changing to be more loving, respectful and inclusive during this shift in consciousness.

Ultimately, we are of no use to others if we do not take care of ourselves. When we focus on ourselves as an aspect of everything, and in knowing that we affect the collective with our change in thought, we become more mindful of our realities and how we are playing out this experience.

In claiming "I am this" or "I am that" we end up separating ourselves from within. Change the word "I" to "We" and see how quickly you change in regards to how you interact with yourself, and others, in your world.

We are collectively one big-energy; and others are simply a reflection of ourselves, so what are the other beings showing you? If you can see anger in another, see where you have anger within. When you can see separation in another, see where you are separated within.

Coming from respect, understanding, and honor with all beings as you respect, understand, and honor your own journey only enhances the shift into unity consciousness. Start to see the universe as a whole and you will become more whole within. It is this aspect of wholeness that shifts lower dimensional beings into the higher dimensions because the more whole one becomes, as they remember they were always whole to begin with, the higher one ascends in frequency.

PART THREE:

CHOOSING YOUR EXPERIENCE

THE HUMAN MIND

"You have power over your mind - not outside events. Realize this, and you will find strength."
- Marcus Aurelius

The human mind is a powerful thing; it can believe anything it wants to. We change our thoughts all the time, and thus change our reality. Beliefs are just collections of thoughts, and the mind controls those thoughts. We give power to our mind, and with that power it can either keep us in a prison of our choosing or it can set us free from our beliefs when we choose to see something different about ourselves and our world. The human who believes in limits is limited. The human who is afraid of death will see death everywhere. The human who sees the good in everything will experience the good everywhere it goes. Pay attention to how you see the world and you can discover the underlying beliefs that shape your reality.

The mental body is in charge of playing the game, but it also takes cues from us and our other bodies of consciousness. Ultimately, we are not our minds. The infinite possibilities in the universe exist right outside of our boxed belief systems. The human aspect has had a limited range of experience over the last few thousand years; it created our boxes and now it is our job to disassemble them. Begin to tear down those boxes as you pick apart your mind, your thoughts, and see just how ridiculous they truly are. The more one can see the more one can change. How can you choose to walk a new path through life if you didn't know that path existed in the first place?

If you don't currently believe that you have the power to change your reality with just a thought, realize that you have already been doing this your entire life. "Psychosomatic," or "it's all in the mind," is a term we use to describe the psychological phenomenon of creating reality with just a thought. Have you ever made yourself sick on purpose to get out of work or school? When I first started working I was under the impression that I had to actually be sick in order to be able to call out from work. So when I really didn't want to go, I would end up getting really sick. I didn't learn until later than people just called out sick to work when they just really didn't want to go, or had something else to do, and not because they were actually sick. Our minds are sophisticated machines: if we believe we need to be sick in order to get out of doing something, then the mental body is going to communicate with the physical body and create a sickness for us to validate that experience.

We don't put two and two together when we want something to happen and when it actually happens. Our universe listens to our deepest desires. If you are really dreading going to school, then maybe your universe sends you a snow storm so you can stay home. If you are super excited for a new date Friday night, then maybe your universe makes everything go as smoothly as possible. But if it is a blind date and you really don't want to go, things are going to happen to either push you to admit you don't want to go, or it will confirm how horrible you thought it would be by bringing you certain experiences on that date.

See what your mind is thinking, and see where you are manifesting those thoughts in your reality. Remember to notice what kind of energy you are putting out into the world because that is the energy you are getting in return.

Whether we realize it or not, thinking happens constantly. There are many unconscious programs running around based on our thoughts and experiences. Has your mom every told you that you'd catch cold if you didn't wear a hat outside? Has this affected your experiences in the winter time as an adult? Would you believe any of your reality if no one ever told you to believe it? One comment from some random stranger we met once as a child could have created an entire series of thoughts, beliefs, and subsequent events based on that comment.

We are shaped by what we allow ourselves to believe in reaction to the holographic programming happening around us. Are your thoughts your own? Or do you believe something someone else has told you as their truth? Knowing how your mind individual mind works will let you override the programs that keep you trapped in those boxes of beliefs.

Everything is just an experience to the mind. It does what it has been programmed to do. If you don't like what you are seeing in your reality, first look at your thoughts about it. The human mind, or the ego, ultimately teaches us that we are not our thoughts. The ego wants an explanation to everything, and will justify its experiences with attachments, expectations, and judgments. The mind jumps at the opportunities to create new realities with each new thought we have about ourselves, each other, and the world around us.

The human aspect can feel powerless to its thoughts at times, but now is the time to break down those thoughts and take control of our realities once again. This new shift in consciousness and all the new upgrades to the programming are allowing a major change in the relationship between all four bodies of consciousness: they are unifying, and they are working together to form a whole new experience for humanity to play with. We get to create the hologram we want to live in now.

Automatic Programming:

Think of the mind as a computer. Most of our thoughts are just automatic programs running in the background. As discussed previously in the four bodies of consciousness, the physical body breathes for us while we sleep and heals itself when it gets injured. Likewise, the mind runs on autopilot most of the time. We wake up, we get dressed, we get ready for the day (or night), and we do this or that as routine programming.

We do so many things out of habit that we have tuned most of our thoughts out. Those thoughts are still running around somewhere in our mental body, and until we consciously choose to stop thinking a certain way or to change our thought about something, then those programs will still continue to affect our projected holographic reality.

Often, the key to our automatic programming is in our gut-reaction responses to events that happen in our life. Let's say that you spend four hours preparing a nice dinner for your friends or family. And on your way to serving that dish your cat jumps in front of your legs and you trip, sending the dish flying across the room. What is your first response? Are you embarrassed that you tripped? Do you get mad at the cat and blame him for ruining your dinner party? Do you get mad at yourself and say you should have been more careful? Are you more concerned about yourself, your cat, or your dinner guests? Are you ashamed to order a pizza so everyone can eat? Do you want to punish the cat but will do it later because you don't want your friends to see? Do you brush off the incident as an accident and make sure the cat and your guests are okay? Now here is the fun question: Why?

We often don't know why we think the way we do. And that is perfectly okay. The point is not to know why we think the way we do, the point is to change our thoughts in every moment if we choose to do so. So what if you were yelled at as a child for breaking a dinner plate or failing to take out the trash according to your parent's timeline. So what if you still don't take out the trash forty years later when your partner thinks you should. Do you think you are lazy and unworthy?

Only your thoughts about yourself matter. So if you don't like your thoughts, your automatic programming, start changing them. We've attached our thoughts and emotions to many things, many experiences, in our lives which have created new codes in the computer program of our reality. The next time a thought comes up that you are not sure why is there, choose to change that program if you want. Whatever has happened in your life is just an experience, a lesson to grow from, nothing more. Become a master of your own reality again by focusing on the thoughts you want to have, and the things you want to believe in, instead of the ones you don't want to experience any longer.

CHANGING THE GAME

"We are shaped by our thoughts; we become what we think. When the mind is pure, joy follows like a shadow that never leaves."
- Buddha

How you see your reality is essentially the reality you get. Our perceptions influence how we interact with the world. Change the words you use every day and your world will change. When the leaves change color and fall off a tree, refocus your energy towards the new growth that will happen as a result, instead of the death aspect. Do you grumble when it starts to rain outside? Do you dread the first day of snow in the winter? Do you sigh when there are too little clouds in the sky? What are you telling your reality when you do the little things you do every day?

Remember that all four bodies of consciousness communicate with one another, and reality is projected from one or more of those bodies of consciousness. Go inward to see why you think the way you do, what emotions you have in the moment, and why your reality is the way that it is.

Have a healthy regard and respect for your thoughts, your mind, your emotions, and your physical body. They are only doing their job, and they continue to do their job well every day. Your different aspects of self take cues from your deepest desires and wishes. Give them the power to create and they will create. Give them the power to destroy and they will destroy.

Appreciate the thoughts you have had, and say "thank you but I am not going to believe that anymore." Appreciate your emotions as they are just responses to your thoughts and belief systems. See how fast your reality changes when you change your mind, and the way you view your mind, your thoughts, your emotions, and your beliefs.

In order to change the game you're playing, in order to get a new reality, we have to realize that we don't have to keep doing things the way they have always been done. That is part of the old programming. Re-write your life story. Become more present and focused on the moment that is happening right in front of you. Beliefs and limits are self-imposed.

Work with your beliefs as if they were limiting your experience and growth in this moment. What can you become when you believe you are limitless? What can you become when you change your thoughts about yourself?

The game is changing whether we recognize it or not. The earth is already doing its part to change our reality as it ascends into 5th dimensional consciousness and shifts our perspectives, completes contracts, and dissolves timelines we don't need to experience any longer. Accept change as it happens and you will re-program yourself to become more open to the kind of change you want to see in your reality.

Only the human aspect doesn't like change. The natural flow of the universe is change because the universe is fluid. Reality is a verb, not a noun. Practice choosing differently in your story. Set your intentions instead of letting your reality set them for you. We are energetic beings playing an energetic game. When we master our own energy, anything is possible.

An Experiment in Thought:

One could argue that thoughts are the basic units of existence. Our lives are made up of all the thoughts we have had over our entire lifetimes, as well as the thoughts of others. Thoughts, after all, are just energy. We spend the same amount of energy making ourselves miserable as we do making ourselves happy. If we think we are getting the same old reality, day in and day out, then that is what we get. But if we can start to believe that we are working towards something new, and that we truly believe that we have the power to change our world, then that is what happens.

It takes constant commitment to change, because our many thoughts and beliefs have been built over long periods of time and have many emotional attachments to them. But change can be done: it happens naturally after all! All things are possible if you believe they are.

According to popular belief, the sky is the limit. However the real limit is our belief systems. Thoughts repeat over time to form our beliefs. Usually our beliefs are inherited through other people: the things we have heard, things we have been told to believe, and the things we have been told not to believe. The human aspect likes control, and will easily accept a new belief when it gets told repeatedly and constantly. If everyone thinks it, it must be true…right?

Here is a good tip: don't believe everything you think. There are still third dimensional programs running around; programs that promote fear, duality, and survival. These programs keep the human aspect in fear mode so that we won't do anything to interfere with its perception of our survival. You are allowed to say: "thank you, but I don't believe that anymore." You may have to repeat it until the program changes, but the program will change.

So let's try at an experiment. Words are the basic unit of thought. What words come up when something happens in your reality? What emotion comes up when you *drop* something? How do you feel when you *fail* a test? How do you react when you *overcook* something? What do you say when your drive-thru order is *wrong*? How you react to a word determines what that word means to you.

Words have power, so start to listen to the words you use in every moment. Words, as aspect of thought, are just energy. Love and fear are the only two forces in the world, and each emits their own vibrational energy. A fun little experiment to try is to write the words *"I Love You"* and *"I Hate You"* on two separate pieces of paper and tape them to two identical bouquets of flowers, or to two glass jars filled with cooked rice. Make sure the words are facing towards the object. See if you notice any differences in how the object functions over time. When something receives words of love it reacts differently than something that receives words stemming from fear. Words do have power, and we have the power to change our words.

DISCERNMENT

"Don't forget: no one else sees the World the way you do, so no one else can tell the stories that you have to tell."
- Charles de Lint

You have all the knowledge you need within in order to determine what types of experiences you want to participate in. We all view our story, our play, our movie, our ride, and our playground however we want to see it.

Discernment is not about judgment. There are no good or bad experiences. Choose to become more conscious in your thoughts, beliefs, and actions. Only you know what is right for you, and only you know your personal truth. Engage with your external environment in a different way than before by asking questions:

Does this apply to my journey?

How often do you experience things that you don't necessarily need? Be aware of the energy you are feeding in the moment. Why do you do the things you do? Are you buying that new video game as a distraction from what you know you should be doing in this moment? Are you eating that piece of chocolate cake because you are hungry or because you are depressed? Do you need to prove who you are to someone else? Why? Pay attention to your energy to determine if an experience truly applies to your journey at this time, or if you need to go in a different direction than originally planned.

Is this of the highest good for my journey?

Are you supporting your journey and/or the journey of those around you? Are you still doing the same old thing hoping for different results? If there is an experience that is no longer serving your highest good, you don't have to participate in it anymore. You have the choice, and the power, to change your mind in any moment and to re-train your thoughts and behaviors to align yourself with your goals. Focus on the energy you want to receive back from your universe like a mirror, and not on the energy you don't want to receive. When we change our thoughts, we change our world.

How much do I want to participate in this?

There are often forks in the road on the path of life. Which path will get you to where you want to go? How long do you want to stay on that path? Everyone is on their own journey, and you don't have to do something the way it has always been done. Listening to other people's opinions on what you "should" or "should not" do is limiting your story. Regain the power of your own story, influence the universe into having the experiences you want to have, instead of letting other people provide your lessons in life based on their story. You can choose to stop participating in an aspect of your story and re-direct your energy to the experiences you want.

What else can I gain from my current story/situation?

At first glance the human aspect doesn't see the whole picture. It forms an opinion right away about a person, place, or thing in its reality. Take a step back and discern your surroundings. Why am I having this experience? What do I need to learn from this experience? Have I learned all I need from this experience, and if so, can I move onto a new one now?

Remember that soul contracts change in every moment, sometimes we fulfill them and sometimes we get an addendum depending on the situation. If you are experiencing the same thing over and over again, try to think beyond the box and see what you have been missing. There are infinite angles in which to discern what is truly happening around you.

Appreciation:

Appreciation is a great tool for discerning what you do and do not want in your reality. Appreciate everything, even the experiences you don't like, because those experiences happened for a reason. You are allowed to say: "thank you but I don't need this experience anymore in my reality." Labeling an experience or a choice we have made as wrong invites that experience to keep happening until we come at it from a more neutral approach. The human automatic programming will judge an experience, but we, as the person behind the curtain, have a choice to tell our mind to knock it off, or not.

In completing soul contracts, appreciation is like signing off on an experience. Appreciate the people who come and go from your life; everyone teaches us something new. You asked that person to play a role, or a part, in your story. You asked them to trigger what needed to be triggered within you. Ask yourself why you are upset, sad, or uncomfortable in your interactions with others. Sometimes we need to walk away from certain experiences. We don't have to put up with anything we don't want to in our lives.

Discern what you need. What are you allowing in this moment? Not many people are aware that we give permission all the time on an unconscious level. Become aware of your permissions on a conscious level and see what falls away from your reality naturally as a result.

Appreciate by listening to your body, your mind, your emotions, and your soul. We show appreciation by directing our energy towards an object; whether that object is a person, an animal, or a thing in our reality. Ask yourself how you can assist your physical body in this moment. Do you need to stop and rest, or do you need to get out and do something? Discernment is simply acting from an awakened observer state. When you take the time to appreciate something, to really notice everything it is doing for you in this moment, or has done for you in previous moments, or will do in future moments, then that something feels appreciated and will assist your journey in the highest good it can provide. If you say: "thank you, but now I want this to happen," this gives your universe a snapshot of your desire to change your reality. We can be thankful for our experiences and want them to change at the same time.

Saying No with Love:

It is okay to say: "no, I am not going to do what I did in the past." The human aspect likes to continue doing what it knows and what is feels is easy until we put our mental foot down. It is only the mind's perception that an experience is difficult change or that our choices don't matter. This is your journey, so stand up for what you want and let other people worry about their own journey.

In order to stay on our path and maintain happiness, sometimes we have to establish boundaries. We are allowed to tell the people in our reality that if they want to remain in our life then they have to come from a place of honor and respect. Require others to take responsibility for their reality as you do yours.

There is no need to save the entire world. Our only responsibility is to ourselves and our individual journey. If other people in your life don't want to respect your choices, or your decision to live a more conscious lifestyle, then that is their issue. You have to decide if you need to move forward on your journey without them.

Since we are energetic beings, we can choose to say no with love. Everyone emits their own energetic frequency, and sometimes we don't want to be around people based on their current state of that frequency. Likewise, other people may not want to be around us if we're working through the emotions of anger, sadness, blame, shame, and guilt.

Our energies attract and repel. You'll find your relationships will change when you start to recognize the energy that is around you. When you love who you are, your energy will reflect that. You can choose how people see you by choosing how to see yourself. If you come from a place of love, respect, and honor for yourself and your reality, others will see you in that light because you honor and respect yourself.

CHOICE, OR FREE WILL

"There is a town where the soul is fed, where love hears truth and thrives, and another town that produces lies that degrade and starve love. Your voice is a small market set between the two towns."

– Rumi

Our souls, or higher selves, designed our lives to a certain point in order to ensure certain experiences for the collective soul body and Source consciousness. Beyond these experiences, we are left to choose and experience life at will, free will that is. Our guides are ourselves in a different dimension, plane of existence, frequency or realm in which they have chosen to help us during our ascension process. Guides, or our angels if you will, show themselves within the little synchronicities of everyday life. There are no demons, only in the minds of man and ego as an illusion of separation and fear from our true nature: pure light and divine love. It is the individual's choice to listen to their intuition, their guides, or not, and to trust in what they receive.

Some choices are made for us, yes, by us in fact, but we, as the incarnation who is reading this book, have the ultimate decision in how we live. Time is an illusion, we exist in multiple dimensions at once: lower, higher, in between and all. We chose to forget this when we were born into a human vessel on a planet someone named Earth. We chose to accept this limiting belief, the lie, that we are mere mortals doomed to struggle and toil away until our vessels decay and ultimately die.

And we can choose now, in this moment of ascension, to do something new. We can choose, in this moment, to create our reality outside the confines of the boxes we once put ourselves in and to usher in a new world for all soul bodies to experience at a higher level of consciousness.

We can choose whether or not we want to enjoy our journey. Most people are not even aware of this choice in their lives. Life isn't hard or horrible unless you believe it is. Thoughts are a choice, and we can choose to think differently about ourselves and the world around us if we want to. If you want the new in your life then you have to ask for it from your universe and then choose to look for it in your reality.

The human aspect will do anything and everything it can in order to not see and accept what it sees as new. The human aspect likes the old programming; that is where it functions best, and where it feels like it is in control. This is not about control anymore. Control is a fear-based program. Overcoming fear takes trust: trust that the universe will catch you when you fall, or when it lets you fall that it is for the highest good of your experience and growth. You can choose how you want to interact with your world.

Everything comes down to choice. Choose what you want to believe. Choose the changes you want to implement in your life's story and show your courage by actually changing. Choose to be happy, or at least choose to start accepting the parts of your story you have no control over. If your car breaks down you have a choice to be angry or to go with the flow with the universe. The more choices you make in a higher vibrations (love, respect, understanding) the more conscious you become.

This is about energy. Which reality do you believe is real? Do you want a different reality? Do you want a new experience? Openness is a state of energy, closed-mindedness is another state. If you are open to new experiences, if you are expecting the new to come into your life, then that is the energy your universe sends you. If you remain closed off to change and stick to the same programs in your day-to-day activities, then that is okay too. Just remember that your reality changes to your choices and your energy in every moment.

Choose to wake up, or choose to stay asleep. Both paths lead to the same destination, for all paths do. Our paths are ours alone to walk, and yet we walk multiple paths at one time, across time, and without time. We walk the same path over (déjà vu) too. Lifetimes converge and diverge; we meet ourselves at every stage and in the beyond after our time is "done" on the Earth as well. Soul families are eternal. We come from Source and we shall return to Source at the point in "time" when we are ready. And by ready I mean when we have experienced all that we set out to and when we have ascended through the cosmic hierarchy of dimensions and frequency.

However you choose to live your life is destined and perfect, so choose what you feel is right, what you feel will make you happy, and what you discern as the highest good for yourself and those around you.

CONSCIOUS CREATION

"Men do not quit playing because they grow old; they grow old because they quit playing."
- Oliver Wendell Holmes

Yes, we can create our own reality. Conscious creation is becoming a master of our four bodies of consciousness again in order to consciously influence and direct our holographic reality at will. This is the opposite of waiting for someone, or something, else to save us. This is not about waiting for things to change in our reality first before we change ourselves. If you want something done, you have to do something.

To create the reality we want, we first must become conscious of our thoughts, feelings, words, and actions. The words we use are constantly reinforcing the energy of our feelings and maintaining an energetic loop of thought. We may want more money but inside we feel poor and undeserving. We may want to find true love but inside we feel ugly and worthless. Pay attention to your underlying programs, for they are they clues to what is being reflected back at you in your reality.

We are creating this reality in every moment for our own advancement in consciousness, whether we are aware of it or not. We create our realities from our thoughts: consciously, subconsciously, and unconsciously. Be a conscious creator of your reality by being mindful of your thoughts, your energy, and projecting the world you want to see and live in.

Realize how much power you've given away in your life by letting your hologram create itself. We are the ones who determine what our priorities are. When we focus on ourselves and creating the reality we want, we become invested energetically into the creation process, and our universe responds in turn.

We control the hologram, and we each have to believe that we can control our own projected realities. The goal of the ascending human is to create a world it can play in with a new set of parameters, rules, and achievements. With practice, we can become masters of our realities again, and turn this experience into something beyond what the human aspect could ever dream of.

Practice playing by creating the scenarios you want in your mind's eye, i.e. the imagination. Daydreaming is a wonderful tool in the creation process. If you can't see it, then it doesn't exist for you. Know your options and discern what you do and do not like about your reality. Whatever you allow your thoughts to do is what you are ultimately allowing in your life.

Do you dream the same thing every day? Can you dream of something different than what you've always done? Reprogram your thoughts, and you will reprogram your world. The human mind can get stuck seeing the same old thing over and over again because this is safe, because change is scary to the ego who is concerned with survival. If we want the new, then we have to look for it and accept it.

Everyone and everything was created by you in this reality. Our intentions manifested physical matter. You created that blue pillow on your couch so you could rest. You created that laptop so you could work. You created window blinds so you could open and close your world at will.

What story do you tell yourself about that pillow, or that teapot, or your dog and cat? Did you buy that pillow because it was on sale and you didn't think you could afford better? Or did you spend a hundred dollars on that pillow because you were afraid of what other people might think about you based on your pillow selection? Do you even need that pillow? We no longer agree to become victimized by our surroundings when we take responsibility for it.

As a conscious being, it's never about another's actions. It is always only about our actions. This is our reality, our hologram, and this is our journey. No one can tell you what works for you in creating your own reality. You can choose how you want to interact with the food you eat and the water you drink. You can choose to believe things are good for you or bad for you.

You can choose to believe what you are doing to your body is right or wrong, and you can believe your world works only in a certain way. Challenge the belief structures you've been operating under and decide what parts feel true to you or not. If you look at the outside world, your hologram, and believe it, then it is yours. Ask yourself questions to determine the kind of reality you want to create, if you don't like the one you have:

What kind of life do I want? What kind of body do I wish to live in and how do I want to look? Do I still want to use money as a means of exchange? How would I like my relationships to be in this moment? What will the Earth look like after it changes? What will the relationship with my cat look like in the new world? What will my relationship with all animals look like?

Fear stops the flow of creation, and fear concretes a certain reality to come forth. Worry is a form of fear. Our imagination is easily transmitted into reality: the universe is paying attention to everything we are thinking and feeling.

Pay attention to the thoughts you are having, and remember that the human mind is a powerful thing. Our energy determines our reality, so if we are focusing on all the aspects of fear in our lives, then we will continue to live in a reality full of fear. But if we choose to start seeing the love in our reality, and become neutral about the experiences we have as being either good or bad, then our reality will reflect a life of love and flow.

Rewrite your life's story, rewrite your programming, and practice consciously choosing your reality in every moment. Letting go of things that no longer serve us or are not in the highest good for our journey is the way of the heart. The human aspect likes to hold onto the old as safe out of fear.

We get to create our reality consciously now, and we do so through our choices: our thoughts, beliefs, feelings, and actions in every moment. Focus on the energy you want to receive, and not on the energy you don't. And most importantly, have fun creating! This is what you came to Earth to do.

EXPANSION AND CONTRACTION

"It's no use going back to yesterday, because I was a different person then."
- Lewis Carroll

Expand your mind and you expand your reality. When we expand, we open up more and more possibilities and potential experiences. We expand by stretching our imaginations past what appears realistic to the human aspect. The limits in our holographic matrix are superimposed: they were created for us as an experience to transcend. If we can put ourselves into the boxes of everyday life, they certainly we can get ourselves out of those boxes. Stretch your mind like a rubber band: when it has been stretched a great distance for enough time it never goes back to its original shape and size. The Earth and our galaxy has been stretching so far in one direction over the last few millennium, that on December 21, 2012 it finally released the tension and snapped into a different reality with new understandings of the previous expansion and a new starting point for the next.

Contraction happens naturally after an expansion, but like the rubber band, our realities never go back to the point they were at before the expansion. The human mind also contracts. We live in a world of infinite possibilities, and we don't have to believe them all, or even experience them all in one lifetime. Simply knowing of these possibilities lets us focus our energy on the experiences we truly want to have in our reality.

There is no fear in the contraction process. We are always expanding, but at times we need to take a break. The human mind is like a muscle: we have to stretch it and use it until it does what we want it to do.

Expand your mind by thinking of as many possibilities for every question you have about yourself and your reality. With new understandings come new truths to resonate with. Only the human aspect limits itself. Only the human aspect fears possibilities because they bring unknown changes to the program. An awakened soul knows it has infinite choice. Those who are asleep aren't aware of the choices they have, and those who are entirely asleep feel like they have no choice at all. The more choices you can see, the faster you can ascend by increasing your vibrational frequency via expansion. Become aware of the choices that are of a higher vibration in your reality. Focus on expanding the possibilities in your reality, even if you don't agree with them. We get to choose what we want to experience and we get to choose what we don't want to experience.

Expansion and contraction are about growth. Experiences add growth. Acknowledge the experiences you have and expand on those experiences for future understandings. The simple thought of expansion is enough for the soul. There is no need to act on anything unless you truly want to. Expansion simply creates new moments. The more dimensions we occupy, the more perspectives we can have. This is why truth changes as we expand and contract. The human aspect has one answer to a question and then it is done thinking. Attachments and expectations to certain realities constrict growth and don't allow for proper expansion. Look at different perspectives, see many ways of being, and determine what feels true for you in each and every moment. Our consciousness is no longer bound to our physical body; we can dream of limitless possibilities and act on them in our realities at will.

125

UNIVERSAL TRUTHS vs
PERSONAL TRUTH

"Three things cannot be long hidden: the sun, the moon, and the truth."
- Buddha

Technically all things are true. Our story is just one aspect of that truth. Truth is constantly evolving with new experiences and new understandings. Truth is subjective, and relevant only to the moment you are in. Nothing is absolute except for the flow of energy and change. The knowledge located in the universe is expansive; expand your options and choose what feels right with you. We get to pick what resonates with us and throw out all the rest. Discern what is true for you, and what is not so true, and get okay with your truth changing as you change. You are allowed to change your mind.

What matters most in this experience is our intuition. We can each share our perspectives on the world and how it works, but ultimately we each have to find our own truth by trusting our gut feelings. If something doesn't see right with you, move onto the next thing. Find what resonates with your heart and you will find your truth. The human aspect doesn't like to listen to the universe, or its higher self. The human thinks it knows best, and will go along with the majority instead of living its own truth. Remember that the human aspect lives in fear; fear of rejection, fear of persecution, and fear of failure from its thoughts and beliefs.

Ultimately truth shows itself through action. Trust your truth and have the courage to change it when it doesn't sound truthful anymore. We are allowed to change our minds. We can live our entire lives in one truth, and then we can experience something that shatters that truth. Choose what you want to believe, and choose how truthful you want to be in your actions. Stretch your imagination to what seems possible over what seems realistic. Trust what you feel when you find new information. Your truth changes just as your thoughts do, so get okay with knowing you are exactly as you need to be in this moment. Knowledge comes through the heart, and this is also where we discern our truth.

It is the individual's journey to discern their own truth. There are universal truths, but ultimately we get to decide if they resonate with us or not. Here are some universal truths to think about:

All is One: everything is an expression of Source, as the oneness from which everything derives from and exists to return to. We are all aspects of Source and we are all connected through it.

Ascension: the world is experiencing a spiritual transformation of consciousness. The entire universe ascends as it rises in vibrational frequency into a new dimension of consciousness, which provides different forms of experience.

Change your thoughts, change your world: the world changes when we bring about a spiritual change within ourselves. This occurs automatically and consciously as reality shifts in response to human thought.

Intuition: our connection with the soul body. Developing intuition provides an essential insight into one's life experiences and promotes a spiritual transformation in achieving personal truth and potential.

Life after death: from the point of view of your true self, your soul body, life is infinite. The physical body is just a vessel in which to experience a form of life, and when we are done we move on to a new physicality. Our essence is eternal; it is just the shell that dies.

Life reflects who you are: our beliefs, thoughts, feelings, and actions create our reality. Life is but a mirror that shows us our true selves, beyond and beneath the perceived layers of external self. As mirrors, we can choose which reflection we want to see in the world by changing our beliefs, thoughts, feelings, and actions.

Our purpose is to experience: each person is unique, their journeys are unique, and the purpose of life is to experience everything we can from that unique point of view. We are expressions of Source as individuals with individual experiences.

Reincarnation: as souls, we can come back to the same planet in order to gather more experience. We will incarnate again and again until we have learned everything we need to over the course of many lifetimes.

Responsibility: as we each create our own reality, we each have a responsibility to the creation process.

Truth is found everywhere: while ultimate truth is found within, we must gather as much information from all kinds of sources in order to determine that truth. With each new understanding our truth shifts to reflect what resonates with us at a certain time.

Unconditional love: this is the true expression of the universe. Unconditional love accepts all as it is, and shares in assistance for the highest good.

With all truth, find what resonates with you and discard the rest. Research everything you can about a particular subject before deciding if it is true for you or not. And be open for changes in your truth. We may not understand something because of our limited viewpoints and lack of information, but when we do understand it, then we can choose if we want to believe it or not. Trust in the energy you receive from your senses; if it doesn't feel right, then it isn't right for you. And that is perfectly okay. Find your truth, and live it. Allow others to live their truth as they see fit as well.

Establishing Trust:

Establish trust by believing in yourself and your abilities. Trust what your heart desires over what your ego mind is telling you. Society tells us to be ourselves, and then on the other hand tells us to be like everybody else.

Discern what is true and what is not true for you and your journey by practicing trust and developing your intuition. Only you know what you feel, and only you know what you need to do from those feelings.

Perform your own lie-detector test to determine where you come from truth. Close your eyes, put your hands on your heart, and say aloud things you know to be true and things you know not to be true. You will feel what you truly believe. Truth feels different from a lie. Notice how your voice changes when you speak a truth and when you don't. Often what we can't say aloud tells us more than what we can say.

Establish a friendship and respect with your body, your mind, and your soul. Feed your body love by saying you love it. Feed your mind love by appreciating what it does for you and your reality. Feed your emotions love by allowing them to exist.

No matter what your vessel looks like, how it functions, how it thinks, and how it feels, your entire light body of consciousness provides the opportunity to experience life.

There are only two forces of truth: doubt and trust. Do you doubt yourself and your abilities? Do you trust that your universe is providing the experience you need in this moment? Do you trust yourself to change your mind and make a new decision when you need to?

Doubt often creeps in when the human mind experiences something it perceives as unrealistic. Automatic programs determine if you are going to succeed or not, simply because you either believe that you will, or you believe that you won't. Reprogram your thoughts, trust that you can change, and believe in that change.

RESPECTING THE JOURNEY

"There are hundreds of paths up the mountain, all leading to the same place; so it doesn't matter which path you take. The only person wasting time is the one who runs around the mountain telling everything that his or her path is wrong."
-Hindu Proverb

Everyone's story is true for them. When we judge another's story, we are actually judging our own. If we don't believe the words that are coming out of someone else's mouth, we really don't trust others to believe us when we speak. Often the human aspect regrets a situation when it realizes the other person was telling the truth all along, and we simply just didn't listen. Honor the need for others to live their story as they see fit. If they lie to you, that is on them, not you. If their intentions are not honorable, that is not your problem. You can choose to be a victim to other people, places and things, or you can choose to come from your own honor and let the world do what it's going to do.

Our only responsibility in life is to the choices we make. Accept the consequences of your decisions and get okay with whatever happens. If you don't like a choice you've made, make a new one. Your choice is your own, and so are the results of that decision. When someone else makes a choice for them, choose to honor their journey as they need to. "I honor your journey. I honor what you are experiencing." This doesn't mean you have to agree with it. And they don't have to agree with your decisions.

We all know what is best for ourselves, and sometimes we get

131

caught up in sacrificing our desires for other people because we think we want to be liked by them, or that we don't want to rock the boat. The boat rocks no matter what you do, so do what you feel is right.

Respect the journey by not imposing on another. The human aspect likes to tell people what to do. Humans like to be in control, and yet often give their own freedom away in the process. One of the hardest things we have to learn is to let others choose their own path. The second hardest thing is to learn to make our own choices with little to no outside influence.

We can't physically, mentally, or emotionally do something for someone else. We can assist and guide them by sharing our own experiences, but it is not our responsibility for what do and what they don't do with that information as it is their choice.

All the love in the world won't "save" somebody from their contracts they have agreed to and the experiences they need to learn and grow from. We each have our own path. The human believes it needs to save somebody, and that somebody needs to let us help them. They don't need to let us do anything if their path is heading in a certain direction.

So what if they don't see life the same way you do? We have to get okay with letting others make their own choices, and living out the consequences of those choices. I realized that I could no longer do anything for anyone when I saw my dad put a gun in his mouth. He didn't pull the trigger, but he chose to play with that gun, and he chose to see how far he could go with that experience. All we can do is express our love and let the people in our lives do what they need to. Assist in love, but don't impose on another.

Honor:

Respect your journey first and foremost, and do what you need to do in every moment. Our needs change in every moment, so be open to that change. Honor that change. Honor your journey as it needs to happen. And honor yourself for who you are and what you need to do in the moment. Practice honoring your journey by being raw, real, and honest with yourself in every moment. There is no need to judge ourselves, our thoughts, or our journeys anymore. That was part of the old programming. Change, and the acceptance of change, is the new paradigm.

Honor is staying true to one's self. Changing our needs based on the perceptions of others is not coming from honor. The human aspect likes to compromise itself; it likes to give its power away by allowing others to make choices for it. Our individual needs and desires are just as important.

What is happening in our reality is important to us as individuals. Honor your story, and honor your journey in every moment. And honor the need for others to come from honor themselves. We can't force another person to come from honor and respect; all we can do is accept them for who they are and honor their need to experience what they need to.

We have a conscious choice in what we allow in our realities. We can allow ourselves to be happy. We can allow ourselves to change. Give yourself permission to not care what people think. Give yourself permission to be happy the way you need to be happy. We each hold the power to change our thoughts, beliefs, and create the reality we want to live in. The trick is not to give ourselves a hard time for enjoying life as we see fit.

Listen to your four bodies of consciousness and determine what you need for your journey. Our job is not to make other people happy or to make changes for other people. Respect the journey, and honor yourself first. Love is energy, and when you come from love for yourself, you will come from love in all aspects of your life and receive love in return from the universe through your reality.

PART FOUR:

FINAL REMARKS

THE MYTH OF SPIRITUALITY

"Reaching for the you that exists beyond all the drama is what the spiritual search is about."
- Annie Kagan

First of all, "spirituality" is not another belief system. There are no rules for becoming, or living, a spiritual life. There is no set system in place that can tell someone they are doing it "right" or "wrong". Remember neutrality? Discovering your own truth and not judging what you find is the journey of life, the path we walk as we learn along the way.

Likewise, being spiritual is not a job or chore one has to do a certain way. There is no to-do list to become a spiritual person, and there is no set way to live life as one sees fit. We don't have to reach a certain mindset in order to ascend. We ascend automatically; our higher selves have that covered. Many people don't even learn they are ascending within their human lifetime. Relax into a more natural state and let life come to you, instead of the other way around.

Most importantly, being spiritual doesn't mean being happy. Happiness is a choice; to look at the "bad" and see the "good" behind it. The more time you take to reflect on yourself and your life, the more unhappy stuff comes up to be released.

As we awaken along our journey, we become more sensitive to the energies around us, including the energy perceived as "negative" or of a lower vibrational frequency than ours. You could be happy one moment and totally sad or angry the next. Happiness is ultimately a choice to come back to after you've gotten all that bottled-up energy out.

Ascension isn't all about butterflies, unicorns and rainbows, although we do get a lot of those here. This journey is about experience. And we have to experience all the emotions, all the thoughts, both good and bad, in order to enrich our lives and understand more at the "end". The journey may be about experience, but it is also about getting okay with that experience. To get okay with all the anger, betrayal, sadness, guilt, loss, and so on, and to flow with what happens in life, is what spirituality is all about. It's about living honestly. If you feel sad, express it. If you feel angry, express it. When it's done, move on to the next experience.

Apocalypse vs Ascension:

The apocalypse is considered to be the end of the world. We have literal interpretations of the apocalypse throughout many religious texts, and other sources like the Mayan Calendar, which ended on December 21, 2012 and caused a slight panic as to what that meant exactly. Like I said before, the world as we knew it did end that day. The Earth was not consumed in fire and brimstone, nor did it get reclaimed by the sea in a major earthquake or flood. The world didn't physically end, just our perception of it. The human aspect got caught up in a certain expectation, a certain way the world is supposed to end, and didn't even realize there was another possibility.

In a sense, we upgraded to Earth 2.0 at the end of 2012. We shifted into a new world, a world one cannot see unless you know to look for it. Centuries before 2012, we had a superimposed matrix of 3_{rd} dimensional duality and survival. We wanted to experience these collectively as a soul body and made a contract with the Earth in order to play out those lower dimensional experiences.

Since 2012, Earth as we know it has been going through an upgrade on a cosmic scale. The game parameters are changing. While other 3_{rd} dimensional planets exist to continue to learn from that particular experience, new incarnations on Earth have signed up to experience the shift through 4_{th} dimensional consciousness and the transition into a 5_{th} dimensional world. Earth was a 3D planet, now a 4D planet, and will be fully into 5D roughly by the end of 2017 (if humanity needs more time to transition into higher dimensional consciousness the planet will accommodate and this date may be pushed back).

We have collectively decided to ascend from 3D to 5D. Many souls have and will continue to opt out of the ascension process; either to go to another planet to continue a 3_{rd} dimensional experience or to come back to earth as a $4_{th}/5_{th}$ dimensional being to help with earth's overall ascension process at a later time. We really don't know until the ride is over which we ultimately choose. Our contracts with the Earth could be complete and we won't need to stick around until the planet has fully ascended. The human aspect is not meant to know.

Physical Ascension

Ascension is basically moving from a lower vibrational frequency, or 3_{rd} dimensional consciousness, into a higher vibrational frequency, or through 4_{th} and into 5_{th} dimensional consciousness, and beyond.

Another way to describe ascension is as the act of the soul moving into the body. We are souls yes, but its participation and interaction with the human form has been limited up until now. The merging of all self-fragments across all timelines, dimensions and realms is the act of ascension.

In a way, the ascension journey is about death. Aside from the occasional monk or Saint, death used to be the only way to ascend as higher beings. That is what the human aspect fears, the physical death. But what I am talking about is the new paradigm for ascension, which is more of a death of the ego while the body integrates with its higher self here on Earth. It is a death of the "old"...the old beliefs, the old constraints, and the old programming. We experience many "mini" deaths as we go through life. And unless it is our path to ascend via the full physical death, we can continue to experience life on Earth throughout the ascension process.

The human aspect fears letting go of the old because it thinks we're losing something; a part of ourselves or a memory. But what we gain by embracing the new is indescribable: a feeling of pure connectedness and unconditional love. That is what ascension is about: pure joy. It's not an overnight process. Everyone on the planet is ascending. Some are aware of it and others are not. Ascension is a continuous process and we really don't have to concern ourselves with whether or not we are ascending at all. That is part of the game: we agreed to ascend and we are doing so in every moment.

The ascension process is mostly automatic. Your higher-self determines the pace. However, as you become aware of your ascension in the physical you can choose to assist the process consciously. Honor the ascension process by acknowledging your needs. Become mindful of what you are doing and what you are feeling. Don't focus too much on the "why."

Frequencies change, dimensions shift, and we can experience all ranges of thoughts and emotions in a matter of moments. Trust what you are feeling in the moment. If you need sleep, then go sleep. If you need chocolate cake, go eat chocolate cake. Assist your body as it assists you in this time. As long as you are coming from love and respect for self and others, you can do no "wrong."

Ascension is merely growth, growth in the spiritual. Some are choosing, or have chosen, to ascend in the physical and assist the shift in group consciousness and the shift in planetary consciousness. Some have chosen to complete their lower dimensional growth and will depart before the planet fully ascends. Some have the option to surpass the need to depart and will continue on with a rapid ascension after their completion of third and fourth dimensional tasks.

We are all on a unique journey, a journey we can't fully understand until we are meant to. The human aspect wants to know, wants to be in control of the process. Ascension, and spirituality, is ultimately about trusting our own truth and going with the flow of our own story.

QUANTUM TOAST AND OTHER THINGS

"But I don't want to go among mad people," Alice remarked.
"Oh, you can't help that," said the Cat:
"we're all mad here. I'm mad. You're mad."
"How do you know I'm mad?" said Alice.
"You must be," said the Cat, "or you wouldn't have come here."
- Lewis Carroll

Quantum toast refers to the phenomenon in which a buttered slice of toasted bread that existed in one dimensional reality was eaten, or consumed, and then re-presented itself in the following moment as an additional piece of toast than previously recognized. When this phenomenon happens, confusion arises in the logical part of the human mind. The mind thinks it just ate two pieces of toast and cannot explain why a third piece of toast presented itself on the plate in a momentary glimpse away from said plate.

The heart of the human knows for certain that this was indeed a third piece of toast that had previously existed in a different dimensional frequency or parallel timeline and crossed-over into the currently perceived dimensional reality. Whether or not one was hungry for that third piece of toast is an entirely different matter. What does matter is that there was no toast on a plate in one moment, and a piece of toast on that same plate in the next moment, or the moment that perceptively came after the moment that had no toast on a plate.

I've also experienced other quantum object phenomenon such as

142

quantum cars, quantum pens, quantum dumpsters, quantum cats, and quantum cereal. Most noticeably was a large dumpster outside a house undergoing construction that was full of broken concrete one morning as I walked my dog around the block, which was not there less than 12 hours later for the second dog walk of the day, but reappeared exactly as I last saw it the next morning about 24 hours after the initial sighting.

Logically one wants to believe the dumpster was replaced and re-filled but not all city dumpsters are alike, especially with graffiti, stickers and other marks gracing each metal container in their own unique way. I felt like it was the same dumpster that was there one moment, gone in the next, and reappeared in the exact same way in the exact same spot as if I was experiencing a déjà vu moment. Perhaps I slipped back into the timeline from the previous morning, or I had received a glimpse into the future yesterday for my experiences today.

Quantum objects ultimately exist to show us that reality is not fixed as we once believed it was. The hologram has hiccups: it resets itself, it switches directions and it flips upside-down, among other things. Anything can happen in a reality that isn't fixed and is based on energetic output and input. The whole point of these holographic "anomalies" is for each of us to accept our reality as is and to go with the flow, quantum toast and all. Anything really can happen in the blink of an eye, or a fraction of that same "time." If you are a fan of the television series *Bewitched*, think of the episode "Endora Moves in for a Spell" (Oct 20, 1966) where Endora and Uncle Arthur had a battle of wills making a house down the street appear and disappear in front of Mrs. Kravitz: in one moment a house was on the corner, and the next moment not. Although shifts in large structures like houses are rare, the facades can change overnight or when someone enters a different dimensional realm temporarily.

Quantum toast is a fun phenomenon, but do you remember when
Alice drank from the little vial that made her shrink in size and
then ate the little cake that made her grow tall? Well, those two
things happen naturally according to the vibrational frequency
we can experience at different times. When we raise our
vibrational frequency really high and really fast, we can feel like
we are floating. The rules of time don't seem to flow like they
should and reality alters based on our own energetic frequency.
Crystals, of all shapes and sizes, raise our vibration when we are
in close contact with them.

I drove 865 miles from Phoenix to Denver with a box of crystals,
including several Andara crystals, in the passenger seat. By the
time I arrived in Denver, thirteen hours later, I noticed things
started to look funny. It was rush hour but I was flowing in and
out of traffic with ease. The last 100 miles usually takes at least
two hours to traverse but as I looked at the clock I realized only
twenty minutes had passed. Pulling up to my mom's house, the
neighborhood seemed quite small, like it was a miniature version
of itself with the streets and houses smaller, shorter, and more
close together. I felt taller than the houses and the giant
evergreens seemed small. I was floating on air and my world
changed accordingly.

The next morning, after coming down from that crystal high, I
took the dog for a walk to discover that now I was the small one.
I had shrunk overnight and it felt like walked forever to get to the
end of the block when it had taken me just a moment the night
before. My vibrational energy lowered from its high the previous
day. When we get really human and vibrate in a low frequency,
we can physically shrink into our surroundings. Other people

notice this change in height and stature as well. So we really do grow taller and shrink depending on our own vibration and the vibration of the area around us.

Play with your reality, and see where the rules bend. Fiction, after all, has a strong basis in reality. Buckle your seatbelts, because the truth about reality is that it's going to get weirder faster and faster as we unravel the thread of the superimposed matrix. As the human mind only experiences what it can perceive, reality ultimately doesn't exist unless you are looking at it. So if a tree falls in the woods, and no one is around to hear it, it doesn't make a sound because it doesn't even exist! Only the presence of an observer can validate the presence of the hologram. Millions of trees exist, and millions of trees have the ability to make a sound, but if a human isn't present, then no one can prove any of it. So how do we even know that reality exists? We don't, at least not for sure. We don't know if anything we believe to be true is really true until the game is over.

FINAL REMARKS

"Not until we are lost do we begin to understand ourselves."
- Henry David Thoreau

We are the only ones who can free our own minds. I can show you the door. I can show you several doors, in fact, and maybe some windows too. But only you can go through them. Only you can change the path you're walking. How do you know which path you are on? Become mindful of your reality, your thoughts, your beliefs, and your actions. When you know what is happening at this moment you can choose to change or to stay the same in the next one.

Reality is fluid. Reality is a verb, not a noun. It changes constantly to the ebb and flow of the merging of individual realities into the collective. When one person changes their reality, by changing their thoughts about it, that ripple effects all other realities it comes into contact with (which is lot if you take into account the nature of energy and the advancements of technology such as the internet).

Ripples make waves, and when one reality collapses others follow; when a new reality is created others are forever changed...the possibilities of reality are limitless. So when you change your thoughts about your reality, you are in fact changing the entire course of thought for all realities simultaneously. Just imagine what we can create with the power we have.

If there is one main thing I have come to understand about the nature of human experience, is that understanding comes afterwards, if at all. The human wants to know the "why" before something happens. During an experience, feelings of anger and confusion can arise because the human wants to know why things are happening in and around our lives. If we get an answer to the "why" it is usually after an experience has taken place.

And sometimes an answer never comes, even after an event has occurred, and sometimes not even after a lifetime of asking the question. One trick to getting through the experiences in life is getting okay with whatever is happening, and finding trust in that what happens is supposed to happen, for whatever reason.

As for what is true and what is not true: we are each living our own truths. But truth is in need of expansion as well. As humans grow, so does their truths. We have to be open to redefining our truths, as we redefine ourselves, in each and every moment, because everything changes moment to moment.

What was true a moment ago may no longer be true now. Especially now in the age of ascension, truths are coming and going at a faster rate. We are evolving rapidly as light-beings, which require new programs and beliefs to alter and fine tune as we move through the ascension process. What no longer serves has to go, including old truths and beliefs. You can let go, and you can believe something new about yourself and your reality.

Life isn't about finding yourself. You already know who you are. It is about remembering again. We are not the person who stares back at us in a mirror. We are not the thoughts that run around in our heads. We are not the tears we cry.

Try not to judge your story. And try not to judge someone else's story. Everyone's story is true for them, just as you know what is true and what is not true for you. Share who you are with the world and let others share who they are with you. No judgments, no attachments, and no expectations.

The mind thinks it knows what it wants, but the soul knows what we need. There are going to be experiences we don't like. There are going to be experiences we don't understand. If we need to complete a task for soul growth, then that is what we'll be directed towards from our universe. Go with the flow, accept the parts of your journey you cannot change, and work on changing the parts you can. With practice, we can become masters of our realities again, and turn this experience into something beyond what we've ever dreamed it could be.

Give yourself permission to go out and play. Give yourself permission to experience this journey fully. This is your playground. This is your opportunity for maximum soul growth. Give yourself the freedom to experience it fully. And remember that you always have a choice. We think we don't have choice, but we do. Become a master of your own reality again by paying attention and making new choices. We are here to play, so play the game you want to play, and play it well!

I honor your journey. I honor your experiences.

Thank you and I love you.

ABOUT THE AUTHOR

Elizabeth Crooks is a writer, author, artist and guide who shares her knowledge of consciousness and the human experience, emphasizing the art of mindfulness and living from the heart. She holds a Bachelor of Metaphysical Sciences degree (B.Msc.) from the University of Metaphysics Sciences, and is a certified Reiki Master with years of energy work experience. When she is not sharing her knowledge through writings she spends her time reading, traveling, walking in nature, creating art, and doodling in love. She is a published author on books pertaining to metaphysical sciences and personal growth as well as coloring books for both adults and children.

For more information, please visit:
www.elizabeth-crooks.com